STANDARDS FOR THE
21st-CENTURY LEARNER
IN ACTION

Related Publications:

Standards for the 21st-Century Learner
Available for download from the AASL Web site.
Packets of handsome full-color brochures may be purchased.
Visit www.ala.org/aasl/standards.

Learning4Life (L4L): A National Plan for Implementation
of Standards for the 21st-Century Learner and Guidelines
for the School Library Media Program
Available for download at www.ala.org/aasl/learning4life.

Empowering Learners: Guidelines for School Library Media Programs
Available for purchase at www.alastore.ala.org/aasl.

The paper used in this publication meets the minimum requirements of
American National Standards for Information Sciences—Permanence of
Paper for Printed Library Materials, ANSI 239.48-1992.

ISBN-13: 978-0-8389-8507-6

Published by:
American Association of School Librarians
a division of the American Library Association
50 E. Huron St.
Chicago, Illinois 60611-2795
To order, call 800-545-2433, press 7
<www.alastore.ala.org/aasl>

Graphic designed by Louis Henry Mitchell.

TABLE OF CONTENTS

ACKNOWLEDGEMENTS

AASL gratefully acknowledges the following:

The AASL Learning Standards Rewrite Task Force (2006–2007):
Co-chair: Cassandra G. Barnett, Fayetteville High School Library, AR
Co-chair: Gail G. Dickinson, Old Dominion University, VA
Eugene Hainer, Colorado State Library
Melissa P. Johnston, Vickery Creek Elementary, Cumming, GA
Marcia A. Mardis, Wayne State University, MI
Barbara K. Stripling, New York City Department of Education
AASL Board Liaison: Irene Kwidzinski, Northville Elementary School, CT
AASL Staff Liaison: Beverley Becker

The AASL Learning Standards Indicators and Assessment Task Force (2007–2008):
Chair: Katherine Lowe, Massachusetts School Library Association
Cassandra G. Barnett, Fayetteville High School Library, AR
Colet Bartow, Montana Office of Public Instruction
Fran Glick, Baltimore County Public Schools, MD
Violet H. Harada, University of Hawaii
Melissa P. Johnston, doctoral student, College of Information, Florida State University
Barbara K. Stripling, New York City Department of Education
AASL Board Liaison: Allison G. Kaplan, University of Wisconsin-Madison
AASL Staff Liaison: Jonathan West

INTRODUCTION

Learning in the twenty-first century has taken on new dimensions with the exponential expansion of information, ever-changing tools, increasing digitization of text, and heightened demands for critical and creative thinking, communication, and collaborative problem solving. To succeed in our rapid-paced, global society, our learners must develop a high level of skills, attitudes and responsibilities. All learners must be able to access high-quality information from diverse perspectives, make sense of it to draw their own conclusions or create new knowledge, and share their knowledge with others.

In recognition of these demands, the American Association of School Librarians (AASL) has developed learning standards that expand the definition of information literacy to include multiple literacies, including digital, visual, textual, and technological, that are crucial for all learners to acquire to be successful in our information-rich society. The new learning standards, entitled *Standards for the 21st-Century Learner*, take a fresh approach and a broad perspective on student learning standards in the school library media field by focusing on the learning process. The *Standards for the 21st-Century Learner* lay out underlying common beliefs, as well as standards and indicators for essential skills, dispositions, responsibilities, and self-assessment strategies for all learners.

These learning standards represent high expectations for today's learners because the skills, dispositions, responsibilities, and self-assessment strategies represented by these standards will provide the foundation for learning throughout life. The standards and indicators will serve as guideposts for school library media specialists (SLMSs) and other educators in their teaching because these skills and dispositions are most effectively taught as an integral part of content learning.

The focus of these standards is on the learner, but implicit within every standard and indicator is the necessity of a strong school library media program (SLMP) that offers a highly-qualified school library media specialist (a term used interchangeably with librarian), equitable access to up-to-date resources, dynamic instruction, and a culture that nurtures reading and learning throughout the school.

Foundation of Beliefs

Strong beliefs among SLMSs undergird the new standards and offer essential points of connection with other educators. The nine beliefs in *Standards for the 21st-Century Learner* feature two core approaches to learning that are embedded in SLMPs—reading and inquiry. Students who can (and do) read and inquire with thoughtfulness and curiosity are empowered to push their own learning to deeper levels and wider vistas.

Implicit within the nine common beliefs is recognition of the importance of skills that lead to productive behavior. Information literacy, the use of technology, critical thinking, and ethical decision making all have a basis in skills and an actualization in the behaviors that students choose to exhibit—from seeking diverse perspectives, to evaluating information, to using technology appropriately, to applying information literacy skills, to using multiple formats.

Finally, the beliefs outline the responsibilities that SLMSs and other educators accept for providing environments that support and foster successful learning. Students must have equitable access to resources and opportunities for learning. The environment must enable students to share and learn from each other because learning is enhanced by a social context. Most importantly, every child in our schools must have access to a vibrant school library.

Organizational Structure

The *Standards for the 21st-Century Learner* and supporting documents have been organized hierarchically to enable many levels of use. An understanding of the overall framework will help SLMSs focus on the level of detail needed to communicate with different audiences and for various purposes.

The highest level is, of course, the four **Standards** themselves. The standards provide a framework for academic and personal learning in today's information-powered world. This level could be used by SLMSs to broaden the perspective of other educators, parents, school board members, and community members about the school library realm—that it goes beyond the simple accumulation of information for class assignments to in-depth academic learning, collaboration, and personal learning.

The second level consists of four **Strands** within each standard: Skills, Dispositions in Action, Responsibilities, and Self-Assessment Strategies. SLMSs are in an ideal position in each school to address the needs and to develop the abilities and attitudes of the whole child, not just the student's academic performance on specified content. The school library media center serves as a laboratory of active learning where students may develop their skills, hone their attitudes, practice their responsibilities independently, and regulate their own learning. SLMSs may use this level of detail when they are communicating about the focus of the library on the full development of each student.

The third level offers **Indicators** under each strand. These indicators delineate actions that students might take to demonstrate their competencies in Skills, Dispositions, Responsibilities, and Self-Assessment Strategies. The indicators are appropriate for students of any age, although the way that students demonstrate their competency will vary by grade level. The indicator level can be used as a framework for a school's program of teaching 21st-century learning skills as an integral part of learning throughout the school.

The final two levels **Benchmarks** and **Action Examples**, are outlined in great detail in the latter sections of this publication. The benchmarks offer specific skills that students can be expected to achieve by grades 2, 5, 8, 10, and 12. The action examples provide models of instructional situations that can be adopted or adapted for teaching the related skills. Both the benchmarks and action examples are grade-level-specific to provide a detailed picture of the development of competencies over years of the school experience. The benchmarks are focused on the development of skills, and SLMSs may use this level of detail to connect and collaborate with classroom teachers to develop specific instructional units that interweave the teaching of skills with the learning of content.

STANDARDS
▼
STRANDS
▼
INDICATORS
▼
BENCHMARKS FOR GRADES 2, 5, 8, 10, 12
▼
ACTION EXAMPLES FOR GRADES K–12

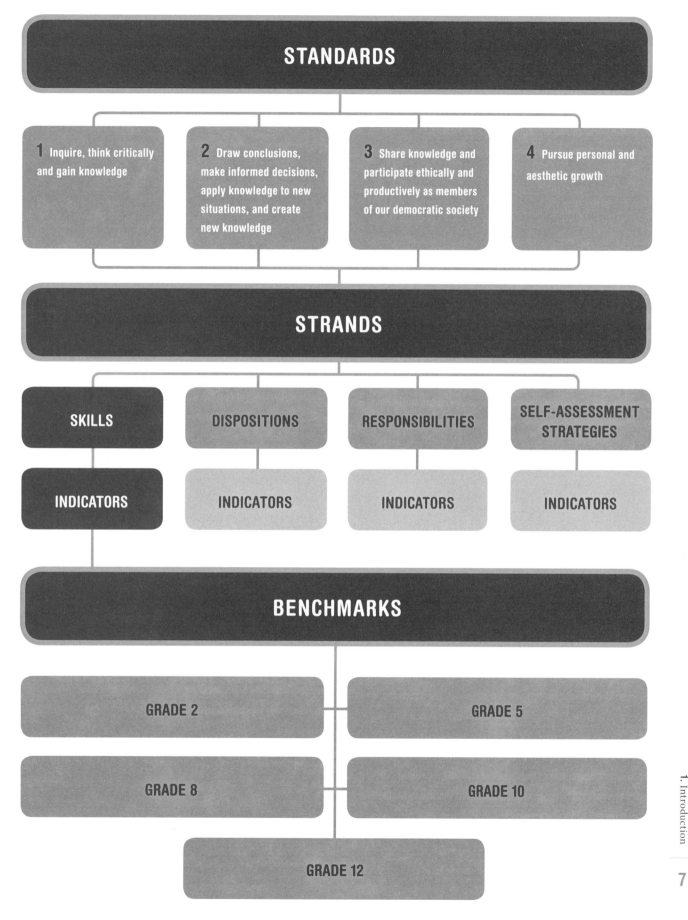

STANDARDS

1 Inquire, think critically and gain knowledge

2 Draw conclusions, make informed decisions, apply knowledge to new situations, and create new knowledge

3 Share knowledge and participate ethically and productively as members of our democratic society

4 Pursue personal and aesthetic growth

STRANDS

| SKILLS | DISPOSITIONS | RESPONSIBILITIES | SELF-ASSESSMENT STRATEGIES |
| INDICATORS | INDICATORS | INDICATORS | INDICATORS |

BENCHMARKS

GRADE 2

GRADE 5

GRADE 8

GRADE 10

GRADE 12

Overview of the Standards

The fact that these standards are focused on academic and personal learning is evident from the flow of learning represented by the standards themselves. Standard 1 addresses the process of investigating and gaining knowledge. In Standard 2 learners are expected to extend that knowledge by drawing their own conclusions, making decisions, applying the knowledge to new situations, and creating new knowledge. In today's interconnected world, learners must go beyond the knowledge they have gained independently because they are increasingly called upon to collaborate and share their knowledge with others while following ethical guidelines (Standard 3). At the apex of the learning taxonomy is the pursuit of personal and aesthetic growth—the motivation and skills to learn on one's own to satisfy internal needs and interests (Standard 4).

Reading, viewing, and listening comprehension is embedded throughout the standards and indicators. Every learner must be able to go beyond decoding to make sense of text, whether the text is traditional print or nonprint, digital, visual, or oral. SLMSs understand that the skills of reading, viewing, and listening comprehension may vary according to the type and content of the text, but all these comprehension skills fall within the realm of these 21st-century standards.

Also integrated throughout the standards and indicators are critical- and creative-thinking skills. Learners are expected to develop skills and strategies at all cognitive levels, described in the original Bloom's Taxonomy (Knowledge, Comprehension, Application, Analysis, Synthesis, Evaluation) (Bloom 1956) and in the revised Bloom's Taxonomy (Remember, Understand, Apply, Analyze, Evaluate, Create) (Anderson and Krathwohl 2001). The highest level in the revised taxonomy, Create, is highlighted in Standards 2 and 3, but creative thinking is also essential to Standards 1, 2, and 4.

Overview of the Strands

Four strands of learning are delineated in *Standards for the 21st-Century Learner* – Skills, Dispositions in Action, Responsibilities, and Self-Assessment Strategies. Any learning is based on Skills; in fact, national standards in every curriculum area outline some of the skills as well as the content for that discipline. These AASL learning standards, however, take a broader approach to the learning process. Successful learners have developed not only the skills of learning, but also the dispositions to use the skills.

Dispositions are the learning behaviors, attitudes, and habits of mind that transform a learner from one who is *able* to learn to one who actually *does* learn. Dispositions can be taught by structuring assignments and learning environments so that they require persistence, flexibility, divergent thinking, or any other learning behavior. Dispositions can be assessed through documentation that proves the student has followed the behavior during the learning process. For example, the student may be asked to document a critical stance with two-column notes: the left column containing information and the right column containing the student's evaluation of this information.

Responsibilities make up the third strand included in the standards. The goal of any educational system is to enable students to emerge as responsible and productive members of society. For that to happen, students must be taught responsibility over the years of schooling. Probably the most effective method of teaching responsibility is to follow a process of gradual release of responsibility, in which the teacher assumes a strong guiding role at first and then gradually transfers that responsibility to the student as the student develops the capacity to assume it. For example, students who are expected to respect copyright and intellectual property rights must learn through a series of experiences how to avoid plagiarism and to rely on their own thinking.

In recognition of the importance of self-regulation in any learning process, the fourth strand is Self-Assessment Strategies. Learners must be able to look at their own work to determine its quality, discover gaps in their own thinking, ask questions to lead to further investigation, find areas that need revision or rethinking, recognize their new understandings, and determine when they need to ask for help. The metacognitive aspects of self-assessment lead to higher levels of thinking and self-monitoring. Self-assessment complements, but does not replace, assessment by the SLMS and classroom teacher.

All four strands are integral to successful learning, but all do not have to be targeted in every instructional experience. To enable SLMSs to connect to the priorities of classroom teachers and content curriculum requirements, a specific continuum of skills within every standard area has been developed for the benchmark grades of 2, 5, 8, 10, and 12.

Although indicators for dispositions, responsibilities, and self-assessment strategies are listed under all four standards, their development is not as aligned to specific standards or specific grade levels as the skills are. SLMSs will find that they can integrate the teaching of dispositions, responsibilities, and self-assessment strategies into instruction in a very fluid and flexible way as appropriate for the learning experience at the time. Dispositions, responsibilities, and self-assessment strategies must be developed through an iterative teaching process conducted over time and through many experiences.

Teaching to the Standards

SLMSs and classroom teachers will find that a collaborative approach to teaching to these standards is most effective because process skills are best learned in the context of content learning, and content is most effectively learned when the necessary learning skills are taught at the same time. SLMSs should not allow difficulties in collaboration (when they cannot find willing partners or the time to collaborate) to block their teaching of these necessary skills and dispositions. Because SLMSs must deal with the realities of their learning environments and figure out the best ways to teach to the standards in a variety of situations, the action examples in the latter part of this publication include samples of instruction in the library at all levels of collaboration.

The importance of inquiry-based instruction is highlighted as one of the common beliefs. Any information processing/research/inquiry model can be used as the structure for the learning process because all of the models have essentially the same phases, as outlined in the learning standards and indicators themselves. The underlying assumption of these learning standards is that students are more likely to be successful in developing the skills and dispositions of learning when they are given opportunities to construct their own understanding and develop skills through guided practice. SLMSs will want to offer direct instruction on a targeted skill, but then scaffold the learning experience so that students are challenged to perform the skill with guidance and then on their own. Although inquiry is a guiding principle for learning, students obviously do not have to work through the entire inquiry process every time they come to the library. SLMSs empower students to be independent inquirers any time the SLMSs teach an embedded skill, disposition, responsibility, or self-assessment strategy. At times, students will be expected to put all their skills and strategies together to complete an inquiry project; at other times, they will learn and demonstrate their competency on the individual skills and strategies necessary for a specific learning task.

Students with special needs and English Language Learners should be expected to learn these skills and given additional support to do so. The social nature of learning—the reality that all learning is co-created—may be particularly valuable for differentiating instruction. Students can be strategically paired and grouped, and the learning experiences structured so that students have multiple, scaffolded experiences to learn a skill by interacting with others. Integrating all learning modalities (reading, writing, speaking, listening, viewing, and representing) is also helpful for students with different learning needs.

Assessment is an important component to these standards. SLMSs have the opportunity to include all three forms of assessment (diagnostic, formative, and summative) into their instruction. Diagnostic assessment, conducted before the learning experience, will reveal students' pre-existing level of knowledge and skills, as well as their misconceptions. Instruction can be adapted to address the diagnostic findings. Formative assessment is easily integrated into any lesson because, when students produce work, it can be assessed for understanding and quality. For example, SLMSs can tell by examining working, annotated bibliographies whether or not students understand how to evaluate sources and select sources relevant to their research questions. Formative assessment is especially valuable for determining students' understanding of process skills because those skills are more evident in the day-to-day work than in the final product. Summative assessment, or assessment at the end of the learning experience, is also useful depending on the skills taught during the unit. If the targeted skill is generating good research questions, the quality of the questions will be more evident from looking at the questions themselves than from looking at the final paper. Rubrics to evaluate final products should include process skills as well as content whenever the skills can be assessed by looking at the final product.

Standards in Action

This publication, *Standards for the 21st-Century Learner in Action*, provides support for SLMSs and other educators in teaching the essential learning skills defined in *Standards for the 21st-Century Learner*. In the latter sections, this publication presents action examples for putting the *Standards* into practice; the action examples are divided into grade-level sections by benchmark grades 2, 5, 8, 10 and 12.

The action examples are just that—examples. They are designed to give a picture of how a lesson or unit might be designed to teach specific skills, dispositions, responsibilities, and self-assessment strategies in the various situations in which SLMSs must operate, from a fully designed collaborative unit to a single lesson taught in the library in a thirty-minute time span. Each action example is based on a scenario that describes very real situations in which SLMSs teach.

Most of the action examples include all four strands to demonstrate the possible integration of dispositions, responsibilities, and self-assessment strategies with skills instruction, but their inclusion does not imply that every instructional situation must address all the strands. The complete examples are offered for illustrative purposes only; SLMSs should adapt the examples to fit their own situations. Every instructional opportunity has merit in helping all our students reach the *Standards for the 21st-Century Learner.*

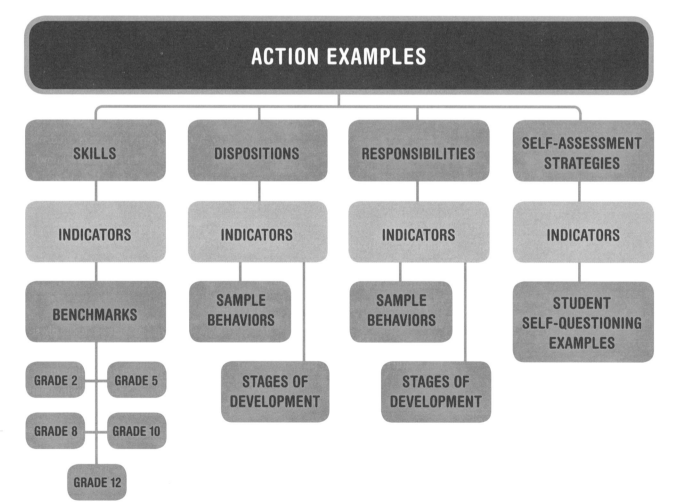

STANDARDS FOR THE 21st-CENTURY LEARNER

American Association of School Librarians

COMMON BELIEFS

Reading is a window to the world.

Reading is a foundational skill for learning, personal growth, and enjoyment. The degree to which students can read and understand text in all formats (e.g., picture, video, print) and all contexts is a key indicator of success in school and in life. As a lifelong learning skill, reading goes beyond decoding and comprehension to interpretation and development of new understandings.

Inquiry provides a framework for learning.

To become independent learners, students must gain not only the skills but also the disposition to use those skills, along with an understanding of their own responsibilities and self-assessment strategies. Combined, these four elements build a learner who can thrive in a complex information environment.

Ethical behavior in the use of information must be taught.

In this increasingly global world of information, students must be taught to seek diverse perspectives, gather and use information ethically, and use social tools responsibly and safely.

Technology skills are crucial for future employment needs.

Today's students need to develop information skills that will enable them to use technology as an important tool for learning, both now and in the future.

Equitable access is a key component for education.

All children deserve equitable access to books and reading, to information, and to information technology in an environment that is safe and conducive to learning.

The definition of information literacy has become more complex as resources and technologies have changed.

Information literacy has progressed from the simple definition of using reference resources to find information. Multiple literacies, including digital, visual, textual, and technological, have now joined information literacy as crucial skills for this century.

The continuing expansion of information demands that all individuals acquire the thinking skills that will enable them to learn on their own.

The amount of information available to our learners necessitates that each individual acquire the skills to select, evaluate, and use information appropriately and effectively.

Learning has a social context.

Learning is enhanced by opportunities to share and learn with others. Students need to develop skills in sharing knowledge and learning with others, both in face-to-face situations and through technology.

School libraries are essential to the development of learning skills.

School libraries provide equitable physical and intellectual access to the resources and tools required for learning in a warm, stimulating, and safe environment. School librarians collaborate with others to provide instruction, learning strategies, and practice in using the essential learning skills needed in the 21st century.

FRAMEWORK

LEARNERS USE SKILLS, RESOURCES, AND TOOLS TO:

1. inquire, think critically, and gain knowledge;

2. draw conclusions, make informed decisions, apply knowledge to new situations, and create new knowledge;

3. share knowledge and participate ethically and productively as members of our democratic society;

4. pursue personal and aesthetic growth.

SKILLS

Key abilities needed for understanding, learning, thinking, and mastering subjects.

KEY QUESTION:

Does the student have the right proficiencies to explore a topic or subject further?

DISPOSITIONS IN ACTION

Ongoing beliefs and attitudes that guide thinking and intellectual behavior that can be measured through actions taken.

KEY QUESTION:

Is the student disposed to higher-level thinking and actively engaged in critical thinking to gain and share knowledge?

21ST-CENTURY LEARNERS

RESPONSIBILITIES

Common behaviors used by independent learners in researching, investigating, and problem solving.

KEY QUESTION:

Is the student aware that the foundational traits for 21st-century learning require self-accountability that extends beyond skills and dispositions?

SELF-ASSESSMENT STRATEGIES

Reflections on one's own learning to determine that the skills, dispositions, and responsibilities are effective.

KEY QUESTION:

Can the student recognize personal strengths and weaknesses over time and become a stronger, more independent learner?

LEARNERS USE SKILLS, RESOURCES, AND TOOLS TO:

1 Inquire, think critically, and gain knowledge.

1.1 SKILLS

1.1.1 Follow an inquiry-based process in seeking knowledge in curricular subjects, and make the real-world connection for using this process in own life.

1.1.2 Use prior and background knowledge as context for new learning.

1.1.3 Develop and refine a range of questions to frame the search for new understanding.

1.1.4 Find, evaluate, and select appropriate sources to answer questions.

1.1.5 Evaluate information found in selected sources on the basis of accuracy, validity, appropriateness for needs, importance, and social and cultural context.

1.1.6 Read, view, and listen for information presented in any format (e.g., textual, visual, media, digital) in order to make inferences and gather meaning.

1.1.7 Make sense of information gathered from diverse sources by identifying misconceptions, main and supporting ideas, conflicting information, and point of view or bias.

1.1.8 Demonstrate mastery of technology tools for accessing information and pursuing inquiry.

1.1.9 Collaborate with others to broaden and deepen understanding.

1.2 DISPOSITIONS IN ACTION

1.2.1 Display *initiative* and *engagement* by posing questions and investigating the answers beyond the collection of superficial facts.

1.2.2 Demonstrate *confidence* and *self-direction* by making independent choices in the selection of resources and information.

1.2.3 Demonstrate *creativity* by using multiple resources and formats.

1.2.4 Maintain a *critical stance* by questioning the validity and accuracy of all information.

1.2.5 Demonstrate *adaptability* by changing the inquiry focus, questions, resources, or strategies when necessary to achieve success.

1.2.6 Display *emotional resilience* by persisting in information searching despite challenges.

1.2.7 Display *persistence* by continuing to pursue information to gain a broad perspective.

1.3 RESPONSIBILITIES

1.3.1 Respect copyright/intellectual property rights of creators and producers.

1.3.2 Seek divergent perspectives during information gathering and assessment.

1.3.3 Follow ethical and legal guidelines in gathering and using information.

1.3.4 Contribute to the exchange of ideas within the learning community.

1.3.5 Use information technology responsibly.

1.4 SELF-ASSESSMENT STRATEGIES

1.4.1 Monitor own information-seeking processes for effectiveness and progress, and adapt as necessary.

1.4.2 Use interaction with and feedback from teachers and peers to guide own inquiry process.

1.4.3 Monitor gathered information, and assess for gaps or weaknesses.

1.4.4 Seek appropriate help when it is needed.

2

Draw conclusions, make informed decisions, apply knowledge to new situations, and create new knowledge.

2.1 SKILLS

2.1.1 Continue an inquiry-based research process by applying critical-thinking skills (analysis, synthesis, evaluation, organization) to information and knowledge in order to construct new understandings, draw conclusions, and create new knowledge.

2.1.2 Organize knowledge so that it is useful.

2.1.3 Use strategies to draw conclusions from information and apply knowledge to curricular areas, real-world situations, and further investigations.

2.1.4 Use technology and other information tools to analyze and organize information.

2.1.5 Collaborate with others to exchange ideas, develop new understandings, make decisions, and solve problems.

2.1.6 Use the writing process, media and visual literacy, and technology skills to create products that express new understandings.

2.2 DISPOSITIONS IN ACTION

2.2.1 Demonstrate flexibility in the use of resources by adapting information strategies to each specific resource and by seeking additional resources when clear conclusions cannot be drawn.

2.2.2 Use both divergent and convergent thinking to formulate alternative conclusions and test them against the evidence.

2.2.3 Employ a critical stance in drawing conclusions by demonstrating that the pattern of evidence leads to a decision or conclusion

2.2.4 Demonstrate personal productivity by completing products to express learning.

2.3 RESPONSIBILITIES

2.3.1 Connect understanding to the real world.

2.3.2 Consider diverse and global perspectives in drawing conclusions.

2.3.3 Use valid information and reasoned conclusions to make ethical decisions.

2.4 SELF-ASSESSMENT STRATEGIES

2.4.1 Determine how to act on information (accept, reject, modify).

2.4.2 Reflect on systematic process, and assess for completeness of investigation.

2.4.3 Recognize new knowledge and understanding.

2.4.4 Develop directions for future investigations.

3

Share knowledge and participate ethically and productively as members of our democratic society.

3.1 SKILLS

3.1.1 Conclude an inquiry-based research process by sharing new understandings and reflecting on the learning.

3.1.2 Participate and collaborate as members of a social and intellectual network of learners.

3.1.3 Use writing and speaking skills to communicate new understandings effectively.

3.1.4 Use technology and other information tools to organize and display knowledge and understanding in ways that others can view, use, and assess.

3.1.5 Connect learning to community issues.

3.1.6 Use information and technology ethically and responsibly.

3.2 DISPOSITIONS IN ACTION

3.2.1 Demonstrate leadership and confidence by presenting ideas to others in both formal and informal situations.

3.2.2 Show social responsibility by participating actively with others in learning situations and by contributing questions and ideas during group discussions.

3.2.3 Demonstrate teamwork by working productively with others.

3.3 RESPONSIBILITIES

3.3.1 Solicit and respect diverse perspectives while searching for information, collaborating with others, and participating as a member of the community.

3.3.2 Respect the differing interests and experiences of others, and seek a variety of viewpoints.

3.3.3 Use knowledge and information skills and dispositions to engage in public conversation and debate around issues of common concern.

3.3.4 Create products that apply to authentic, real-world contexts.

3.3.5 Contribute to the exchange of ideas within and beyond the learning community.

3.3.6 Use information and knowledge in the service of democratic values.

3.3.7 Respect the principles of intellectual freedom.

3.4 SELF-ASSESSMENT STRATEGIES

3.4.1 Assess the processes by which learning was achieved in order to revise strategies and learn more effectively in the future.

3.4.2 Assess the quality and effectiveness of the learning product.

3.4.3 Assess own ability to work with others in a group setting by evaluating varied roles, leadership, and demonstrations of respect for other viewpoints.

4

Pursue personal and aesthetic growth.

4.1 SKILLS

4.1.1 Read, view, and listen for pleasure and personal growth.

4.1.2 Read widely and fluently to make connections with self, the world, and previous reading.

4.1.3 Respond to literature and creative expressions of ideas in various formats and genres.

4.1.4 Seek information for personal learning in a variety of formats and genres.

4.1.5 Connect ideas to own interests and previous knowledge and experience.

4.1.6 Organize personal knowledge in a way that can be called upon easily.

4.1.7 Use social networks and information tools to gather and share information.

4.1.8 Use creative and artistic formats to express personal learning.

4.2 DISPOSITIONS IN ACTION

4.2.1 Display curiosity by pursuing interests through multiple resources.

4.2.2 Demonstrate motivation by seeking information to answer personal questions and interests, trying a variety of formats and genres, and displaying a willingness to go beyond academic requirements.

4.2.3 Maintain openness to new ideas by considering divergent opinions, changing opinions or conclusions when evidence supports the change, and seeking information about new ideas encountered through academic or personal experiences.

4.2.4 Show an appreciation for literature by electing to read for pleasure and expressing an interest in various literary genres.

4.3 RESPONSIBILITIES

4.3.1 Participate in the social exchange of ideas, both electronically and in person.

4.3.2 Recognize that resources are created for a variety of purposes.

4.3.3 Seek opportunities for pursuing personal and aesthetic growth.

4.3.4 Practice safe and ethical behaviors in personal electronic communication and interaction.

4.4 SELF-ASSESSMENT STRATEGIES

4.4.1 Identify own areas of interest.

4.4.2 Recognize the limits of own personal knowledge.

4.4.3 Recognize how to focus efforts in personal learning.

4.4.4 Interpret new information based on cultural and social context.

4.4.5 Develop personal criteria for gauging how effectively own ideas are expressed.

4.4.6 Evaluate own ability to select resources that are engaging and appropriate for personal interests and needs.

The *Standards for the 21st-Century Learner*, published in 2007 by AASL (©2007 by the American Library Association), is available for download at www.ala.org/aasl/standards. Bundles of twelve full-color pamphlets are available for purchase from the ALA store at www.ala.org or by calling 866-SHOP ALA.

2 SKILLS

Defining Skills in 21st-Century Learning

The demands of the twenty-first century require learners to develop essential information literacy skills to evaluate and make sense of the rapidly proliferating, but often biased and inaccurate, volume of information being published. The "text" of information is presented in many different formats, and learners must develop the skills of multiple literacies (print, digital, media, visual) to determine the intended meaning and to understand it in context. In addition, learners must use critical- and creative-thinking skills to transform the information that they gather into organized knowledge that they can use to make decisions, draw conclusions, and create new knowledge. Learners must develop social learning skills as well, so that they can learn from the diverse perspectives of others and participate productively in their community of learners.

Although schools may define a body of knowledge for students to acquire during their educational experience, no learner will be prepared for successful participation in school or society without also developing the skills of learning and the ability to adapt those skills to any context and for any reason, both academic and personal.

Skills and the Learning Process

The power of inquiry-based learning is explicitly recognized as one the common beliefs underlying the *Standards for the 21st-Century Learner.* Inquiry is defined as a stance toward learning in which the learners themselves are engaged in asking questions and finding answers, not simply accumulating facts (presented by someone else) that have no relation to previous learning or new understanding. Inquiry follows a continuum of learning experiences, from simply discovering a new idea or an answer to a question, to following a complete inquiry process. A number of inquiry-process models include the same progression. Learners begin by recognizing what they already know and acquiring enough background information to generate questions for investigation. Using their questions to frame their investigations, learners apply the skills needed to determine accurate answers, generate new ideas and interpretations, and make appropriate decisions and conclusions. To complete the inquiry cycle, students express their new understandings, apply them to new situations, and reflect on their own learning process. Learners do not have to complete a full inquiry cycle to be engaged in inquiry-based learning. Any time they are questioning, finding answers, discovering new ideas, and constructing their own meaning they are drawing upon their skills of inquiry.

The skills required for inquiry run the gamut from low-level, fact-location skills to high-level synthesis, evaluation, and creation skills. Students of all ages should be expected to think while they are learning; thinking is not a luxury reserved for the most-skilled or older students. In all cases, however, students should apply the thinking and inquiry skills in the context of some content that they are learning. The skills will enhance the learning of content; the content will make the learning of skills more meaningful and important.

Teaching for Skills

The skills for 21st-century learning are best taught through an approach in which the teacher guides the learners to construct their own understandings and to apply these understandings to any learning experience. One model of instruction that has been used successfully (because it combines direct instruction with independent practice) is a four-step lesson design:

1) direct instruction of the specific skill to be learned (in context of a topic being studied)

2) modeling and guided practice so that learners have an opportunity to see the skill as it is applied successfully

3) independent practice, with learners applying the skill to their own topics

4) reflection and sharing when the learners look at their own application of the skill and determine how well it worked

The acquisition of learning skills is complex and developmental. Students cannot be expected to learn every skill necessary to complete every phase of the learning process during every unit of instruction. SLMSs and teachers guide students to successful learning experiences by teaching identified skills and scaffolding other necessary skills. For example, if an SLMS has decided to teach students to evaluate websites during one particular unit, then the SLMS may choose to provide the sites to be evaluated, rather than teaching students to develop search strategies and skills. The development of search strategies would be taught during another unit.

Because the skills of 21st-century learning must be developed over time, SLMSs may want to design a curriculum plan for teaching the skills in a coherent way across the years of schooling. This plan must be integrated with content-area curricula to match appropriate skills with classroom content and to ensure that the skills are always taught in context. Sample integrated lessons for many of the skills are included in the action examples in the latter part of this publication.

To facilitate the coherent and continuous development of 21st-century skills, specific benchmarks to be achieved by grades 2, 5, 8, 10, and 12 have been identified for every skills indicator under all four standards. The competencies to be achieved by grade 12 represent the important lifelong-learning skills that students will need to succeed at higher levels of education, in the workplace, and as productive members of society.

The following charts show a developmental approach to each of the skills covered in the four standards. As SLMSs work with the students in their schools, they will differentiate their instruction based on the previous experience and skill level of their students to both challenge and support all their students to reach their highest levels of competency. In some cases SLMSs may have to review or re-teach skills designated for a lower grade; in other situations, students may be ready to move to more complex skills designated for grade levels above their own. In all cases students should be able to build on the skills they have acquired to develop more sophisticated and complex skills and strategies.

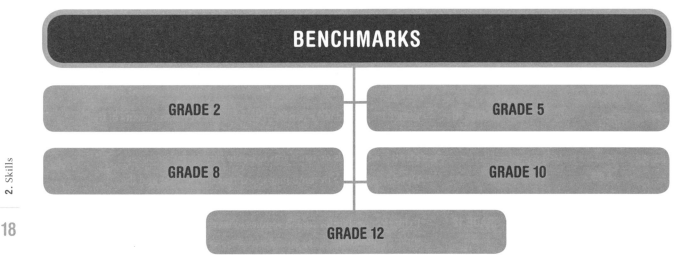

STANDARD 1: Inquire, think critically, and gain knowledge.

STRAND 1.1: SKILLS

INDICATOR 1.1.1:

Follow an inquiry-based process in seeking knowledge in curricular subjects, and make the real-world connection for using this process in own life.

GRADE-LEVEL BENCHMARKS

GRADE 2 – Form simple questions and begin to explore ways to answer them.

GRADE 5 – Generate questions and practice different ways to locate and evaluate sources that provide needed information.

GRADE 8 – Use a critical-thinking process that involves asking questions, investigating the answers, and developing new understandings for personal or academic independent-learning activities.

GRADE 10 – With guidance use an inquiry-based process for expanding content knowledge, connecting academic learning with the real world and pursuing personal interests.

GRADE 12 – Independently and systematically use an inquiry-based process to deepen content knowledge, connect academic learning with the real world, pursue personal interests, and investigate opportunities for personal growth.

INDICATOR 1.1.2:

Use prior and background knowledge as context for new learning.

GRADE-LEVEL BENCHMARKS

GRADE 2 – Connect ideas to own interests.
 – Identify one or two keywords about a topic, problem, or question.
 – Share what is known about a topic, problem, or question.

GRADE 5 – Connect ideas or topics to their own interests.
 – Articulate what is known about a topic, problem or question.
 – With guidance generate a list of keywords for an inquiry-based project.
 – Identify and use appropriate sources to acquire background information.
 – Predict answers to inquiry questions based on background knowledge and beginning observations or experiences.

GRADE 8 – State and support what is known about a topic, problem, or question, and make connections to prior knowledge.
 – Observe and analyze an experience, demonstration, or source that introduces a topic, problem, or question to gather background information.

GRADE 10 – Read background information to discover the key components of the problem or question.
 – Identify keywords or synonyms to use in further research.
 – Develop a schema or mind map to express the big idea and the relationships among supporting ideas and topics of interest.

GRADE 12 – Explore general information sources to increase familiarity with the topic or question.

(continues on page 20)

(continued from page 19)

- Review the initial information need to develop, clarify, revise, or refine the question.

- Compare new background information with prior knowledge to determine direction and focus of new learning.

INDICATOR 1.1.3:

Develop and refine a range of questions to frame the search for new understanding.

GRADE-LEVEL BENCHMARKS

GRADE 2
- Formulate questions related to listening activities.
- Ask "I wonder" questions about the topic, question, or problem.

GRADE 5
- With guidance formulate questions about the topic.
- Assess questions to determine which can be answered by simple facts, which cannot be answered, and which would lead to an interesting inquiry.
- Revise the question or problem as needed to arrive at a manageable topic.

GRADE 8
- Write questions independently based on key ideas or areas of focus.
- Determine what information is needed to support the investigation and answer the questions.
- Analyze what is already known, or what is observed or experienced, to predict answers to inquiry questions.
- Refine questions depending on the type of information needed (for example, overview, big idea, specific detail, cause and effect, comparison).

GRADE 10
- Generate specific questions to focus the purpose of the research.
- Develop and refine the topic, problem, or question independently to arrive at a worthy and manageable topic.
- Formulate questions to collect the needed information to validate or contest a thesis statement.
- Design questions that systematically test a hypothesis or validate a thesis statement.
- Refine questions to provide a framework for the inquiry and to fulfill the purpose of the research.

GRADE 12
- Recognize that the purpose of the inquiry determines the type of questions and the type of thinking required (for example, an historical purpose may require taking a position and defending it).
- Explore problems or questions for which there are multiple answers or no "best" answer.
- Review the initial information need to clarify, revise, or refine the questions.

INDICATOR 1.1.4:

Find, evaluate, and select appropriate sources to answer questions.

GRADE-LEVEL BENCHMARKS

GRADE 2
- Understand the basic organizational structure of books.
- Distinguish between fiction and nonfiction books.
- Understand that the library has an organizational scheme.
- Select and use appropriate sources, including picture dictionaries, beginning encyclopedias, magazines, maps, and globes, to answer questions.

GRADE 5
- Understand the library's organizational scheme and what main topics are included in each section.
- Select and use appropriate sources, including specialized reference sources and databases, to answer questions.
- Use multiple resources, including print, electronic, and human, to locate information.
- Use the organizational structure of a book (for example, table of contents, index, chapter headings) to locate information to answer questions.
- Use text features and illustrations to decide which resources are best to use and why.

GRADE 8
- Recognize the organization and use of special sections in the library (for example, reference, reserve books, paperbacks).
- Locate appropriate nonfiction resources by using the library's classification scheme.
- Evaluate sources based on criteria such as copyright date, authority of author or publisher, comprehensiveness, readability, and alignment with research needs.
- Select a variety of credible sources in different formats relevant to research needs.

GRADE 10
- Identify and prioritize possible sources of information based on specific information needs and strengths of different information formats.
- Use specialized reference materials to find specific and in-depth information.
- Use both primary and secondary sources.
- Evaluate sources based on criteria such as copyright date, authority of author or publisher, depth of coverage, and relevance to research questions.

GRADE 12
- Identify the value of and differences among potential resources in a variety of formats.
- Use various search systems to retrieve information in a variety of formats.
- Seek and use a variety of specialized resources available from libraries, the Web, and the community.
- Describe criteria used to make resource decisions and choices.

INDICATOR 1.1.5:
Evaluate information found in selected sources on the basis of accuracy, validity, appropriateness for needs, importance, and social and cultural context.

GRADE-LEVEL BENCHMARKS

GRADE 2
- Recognize and use facts that answer specific questions.
- Interpret information represented in pictures, illustrations, and simple charts.

GRADE 5
- Skim/scan to locate information that is appropriate to age and ability level.
- Identify facts and details that support main ideas.
- Evaluate facts for accuracy.
- Distinguish between fact and opinion.

(continues on page 22)

(continued from page 21)

– Interpret information taken from maps, graphs, charts, and other visuals.

– Select information to answer questions or solve a problem.

GRADE 8
– Recognize that information has a social or cultural context based in currency, accuracy, authority, and point of view.

– Evaluate and select information based on usefulness, currency, accuracy, authority, and point of view.

GRADE 10
– Recognize that knowledge can be organized into disciplines that influence the way information is presented and use this understanding to effectively access information.

– Evaluate information from a variety of social or cultural contexts, based on currency, accuracy, authority, and point of view.

GRADE 12
– Evaluate historical information for validity of interpretation, and scientific information for accuracy and reliability of data.

– Recognize the social, cultural, or other context within which the information was created and explain the impact of context on interpreting the information.

– Use consciously selected criteria to determine whether the information contradicts or verifies information from other sources.

INDICATOR 1.1.6:

Read, view, and listen for information presented in any format (e.g., textual, visual, media, digital) in order to make inferences and gather meaning.

GRADE-LEVEL BENCHMARKS

GRADE 2
– Use simple note-taking strategies as demonstrated by SLMS.

– Write, draw or verbalize the main idea and supporting details.

GRADE 5
– Use various note-taking strategies (for example, outlining, questioning the text, highlighting, graphic organizers).

– Paraphrase or summarize information in various formats.

– Draw conclusions based on facts and premises.

GRADE 8
– Evaluate, paraphrase, and summarize information in various formats

– Use both facts and opinions responsibly by identifying and verifying them.

GRADE 10
– Take notes using one or more note-taking strategies, including reflecting on the information (for example, graphic organizers, two-column notes).

– Categorize information; add new categories as necessary.

– Interpret information presented in various formats.

GRADE 12
– Restate concepts in their own words and select appropriate data accurately.

– Integrate new information presented in various formats with previous information or knowledge.

– Analyze initial synthesis of findings and construct new hypotheses or generalizations if warranted.

– Challenge ideas represented and make notes of questions to pursue in additional sources.

INDICATOR 1.1.7:

Make sense of information gathered from diverse sources by identifying misconceptions, main and supporting ideas, conflicting information, and point of view or bias.

GRADE-LEVEL BENCHMARKS

GRADE 2
– Summarize or retell key points.

GRADE 5
– Recognize when facts from two different sources conflict and seek additional sources to verify accuracy.
– Recognize their own misconceptions when new information conflicts with previously held opinions.

GRADE 8
– Seek more than one point of view by using diverse sources.
– Explain the effect of different perspectives (points of view) on the information.

GRADE 10
– Identify presence of bias and explain the effect on the information presented.
– Counter the effect of bias on the accuracy and reliability of information by actively pursuing a balanced perspective.

GRADE 12
– Create a system to organize the information.
– Analyze the structure and logic of supporting arguments or methods.
– Analyze information for prejudice, deception, or manipulation.
– Investigate different viewpoints encountered, and determine whether and how to incorporate or reject these viewpoints.
– Compensate for the effect of point of view and bias by seeking alternative perspectives.

INDICATOR 1.1.8:

Demonstrate mastery of technology tools for accessing information and pursuing inquiry.

GRADE-LEVEL BENCHMARKS

GRADE 2
– Recognize the purpose of the online catalog to locate materials.
– Use online encyclopedias and magazine databases with guidance.

GRADE 5
– Search an online catalog to locate materials.
– Use selected websites and periodical databases to find appropriate information.
– Use selected search engines to find appropriate information.
– Use software or online tools to record and organize information.

GRADE 8
– Use technology resources such as online encyclopedias, online databases, and Web subject directories, to locate information.
– Implement keyword search strategies.
– Select and use grade-level-appropriate electronic reference materials and teacher-selected websites to answer questions.
– Use a variety of search engines to do advanced searching.

GRADE 10
– Use a range of electronic resources efficiently, effectively, and safely by applying a variety of search and evaluation strategies.
– Use social tools to demonstrate and share learning.

(continues on page 24)

(continued from page 23)

GRADE 12	– Select the most appropriate technologies to access and retrieve the needed information.
	– Use various technologies to organize and manage the information selected.
	– Create their own electronic learning spaces by collecting and organizing links to information resources, working collaboratively, and sharing new ideas and understandings with others.

INDICATOR 1.1.9:

Collaborate with others to broaden and deepen understanding.

GRADE-LEVEL BENCHMARKS

GRADE 2	– Listen to others with respect.
	– Share knowledge and ideas with others by discussion and listening.
GRADE 5	– Work in teams to produce original works or solve problems.
	– Respect others' opinions through active listening and questioning.
GRADE 8	– Work in self-managed teams to understand concepts and to solve problems.
	– Offer information and opinion at appropriate times in group discussions.
	– Encourage team members to share ideas and opinions.
GRADE 10	– Seek ideas and opinions from others.
	– Respect and help groups find and incorporate diverse ideas.
	– Describe ideas of others accurately.
	– Help to organize and integrate contributions of all group members into products.
GRADE 12	– Model social skills and character traits that advance a team's ability to identify issues and problems, and to work together on solutions and products.
	– Design and implement projects that include participation from diverse groups.

STANDARD 2: Draw conclusions, make informed decisions, apply knowledge to new situations, and create new knowledge.

STRAND 2.1: SKILLS

INDICATOR 2.1.1:

Continue an inquiry-based research process by applying critical-thinking skills (analysis, synthesis, evaluation, organization) to information and knowledge in order to construct new understandings, draw conclusions, and create new knowledge.

GRADE-LEVEL BENCHMARKS

GRADE 2
– Answer the question, "What is this mostly about?"
– Find facts to answer questions in more than one source.
– Note similarities and differences in information from different sources.
– Identify supporting details.

GRADE 5
– Use different clues (placement in text, signal words, focal point of illustration) to determine important ideas in illustrations and text.
– Identify facts and details that support main ideas.
– Restate and respond with detailed answers to factual questions.
– Find similar big ideas in more than one source.
– With guidance make inferences.

GRADE 8
– Assess the importance of ideas by comparing their treatment across texts.
– Identify main ideas and find supporting examples, definitions, and details.
– Analyze different points of view discovered in different sources.
– Determine patterns and discrepancies by comparing and combining information available in different sources.
– Interpret information and ideas by defining, classifying, and inferring from information in text.

GRADE 10
– Identify main, supporting, and conflicting information using multiple sources to support interpretation or point of view.
– Make and explain inferences about main ideas.
– Critically examine and analyze relevant information from a variety of sources to discover relationships and patterns among ideas.
– If discrepancy in points of view is discovered, continue research until the discrepancy is resolved.

GRADE 12
– Build a conceptual framework by synthesizing ideas gathered from multiple texts.
– Resolve conflicting evidence or clarify reasons for differing interpretations of information and ideas.

INDICATOR 2.1.2:

Organize knowledge so that it is useful.

GRADE-LEVEL BENCHMARKS

GRADE 2
– Demonstrate simple organizational skills such as sorting and categorizing.
– Organize information into different forms (charts, drawings).

GRADE 5
– Organize notes and ideas to form responses to questions
– Organize the information in a way that is appropriate for the assignment or question.
– Use common organizational patterns (chronological order, main idea with supporting ideas) to make sense of information.

(continues on page 26)

(continued from page 25)

GRADE 8	– Combine and categorize information by using an outline or semantic web to show connections among ideas.
	– Use common organizational patterns (chronological order, cause and effect, compare/contrast) to organize information and draw conclusions.
GRADE 10	– Use appropriate organizational patterns (cause and effect, chronological order, compare/contrast) to capture point of view and draw conclusions.
	– Experiment with devising their own organizational structures.
GRADE 12	– Organize information independently, deciding the structure based on the relationships among ideas and general patterns discovered.

INDICATOR 2.1.3:

Use strategies to draw conclusions from information and apply knowledge to curricular areas, real-world situations, and further investigations.

GRADE-LEVEL BENCHMARKS

GRADE 2	– Complete a graphic organizer using concepts that were learned during the inquiry experience.
	– Compare new ideas with what was known at the beginning of the inquiry.
	– With guidance make inferences regarding the topic at the conclusion of a theme or research project.
	– With guidance, draw a conclusion about the main idea.
GRADE 5	– Review ideas held at beginning of inquiry and reflections captured during note taking.
	– Match information found with questions and predictions.
	– Make inferences about the topic at the conclusion of a research project.
	– Draw a conclusion about the main idea.
	– Identify connections to the curriculum and real world.
GRADE 8	– Review prior knowledge and reflect on how ideas changed with more information.
	– Compare information found to tentative thesis or hypothesis; revisit or revise hypothesis as appropriate.
	– Draw conclusions based on explicit and implied information.
	– Form opinions and judgments backed up by supporting evidence.
GRADE 10	– Draw clear and appropriate conclusions supported by evidence and examples.
	– Combine ideas and information to develop and demonstrate new understanding.
	– Recognize multiple causes for same issues or events.
	– Apply strategies for making personal and real world connections with information.
GRADE 12	– Combine information and inferences to draw conclusions and create meaning.
	– Develop their own points of view and support with evidence.
	– Present different perspectives with evidence for each.
	– Apply new knowledge to real-world issues and problems.

INDICATOR 2.1.4:

Use technology and other information tools to analyze and organize information.

GRADE-LEVEL BENCHMARKS

GRADE 2
– Use word processing and drawing tools to create written product.

GRADE 5
– Use word processing, drawing, presentation, graphing, and other productivity tools to illustrate concepts and convey ideas.

GRADE 8
– Identify and apply common productivity tools and features such as menus and toolbars to plan, create, and edit word processing documents, spreadsheets, and presentations.
– Use interactive tools to participate as a group in analyzing and organizing information.

GRADE 10
– Use web-based and other technology tools to show connections and patterns in the ideas and information collected.
– Identify and apply common utilities (for example, spellchecker and thesaurus for word processing; formulas and charts in spreadsheets; and pictures, movies, sound, and charts in presentation tools) to enhance communication to an audience, promote productivity and support creativity.

GRADE 12
– Display important connections among ideas by using common productivity tools to categorize and analyze information.
– Use locally available and web-based interactive presentation and production tools to enhance creativity in effectively organizing and communicating information.

INDICATOR 2.1.5:

Collaborate with others to exchange ideas, develop new understandings, make decisions, and solve problems.

GRADE-LEVEL BENCHMARKS

GRADE 2
– Share information and ideas with others by discussion and listening.
– Work in groups to create, share and evaluate simple information products (poster, diorama).

GRADE 5
– Express their own ideas appropriately and effectively while working in groups to identify and resolve information problems.
– Work in groups to create and evaluate pictures, images, and charts for word processed reports and electronic presentations.

GRADE 8
– Participate in problem-solving process with group.
– Work collaboratively in using technology to meet information needs.
– Pay attention to copyright provisions, work in groups to import and manipulate pictures, images, and charts in documents, spreadsheets, presentations, webpages, and other creative products and presentations that effectively communicate new knowledge.
– Work in groups to evaluate products and presentations.

GRADE 10
– Participate in discussions to analyze information problems to suggest solutions.
– Work with others to select, organize, and integrate information and ideas from a variety of sources and formats.
– Use online environments or other collaborative tools to facilitate design and development of materials, models, publications, and presentations.
– Apply utilities to edit pictures, images, and charts while complying with all copyright provisions.

(continues on page 28)

(continued from page 27)

GRADE 12	– Collaborate locally and remotely with peers, experts, and others to collect, produce, and share information.
	– Work with others to solve problems and make decisions on issues, topics, and themes being investigated.

INDICATOR 2.1.6:

Use the writing process, media and visual literacy, and technology skills to create products that express new understandings.

GRADE-LEVEL BENCHMARKS

GRADE 2	– Create a product with a beginning, middle, and end.
	– Use basic grammar conventions.
	– Incorporate writing and oral skills to develop a product or performance.
	– Use pictures to communicate new information and ideas.
	– Revise work with peer or teacher guidance.
GRADE 5	– Follow steps of the writing/creation process: prewriting, drafting, revising, editing, and publishing.
	– Identify the audience and purpose before selecting a format for the product.
	– Experiment with text and visual media to create products.
	– Edit drafts based on feedback.
	– Check for correctness, completeness, and citation of sources.
GRADE 8	– Use prewriting to discover alternate ways to present conclusions.
	– Select presentation form based on audience and purpose.
	– Draft the presentation/product following an outline of ideas and add supporting details.
	– Create products that incorporate writing, visuals, and other forms of media to convey message and main points.
	– Assess and edit for grammar, visual impact, and appropriate use of media.
	– Cite all sources using correct bibliographic format.
GRADE 10	– Select the presentation/product to effectively communicate and support a purpose, argument, point of view, or interpretation.
	– Express ideas through creative products in a variety of formats.
	– Revise work based on ongoing self-assessment and feedback from teachers and peers.
	– Edit for grammar, language conventions, and style.
	– Cite all sources and use specified citation formats.
GRADE 12	– Use the most appropriate format to clearly communicate ideas to targeted audiences.
	– Assess how tone and choice of language impact content in a range of media.
	– Analyze how composition and placement of visual images influence the message.
	– Apply various technological skills to create performances and products.
	– Cite ideas and direct quotes using official style formats.
	– Employ various strategies for revising and reviewing their own work.

STANDARD 3: Share knowledge and participate ethically and productively as members of our democratic society.

STRAND 3.1: SKILLS

INDICATOR 3.1.1:
Conclude an inquiry-based research process by sharing new understandings and reflecting on the learning.

GRADE-LEVEL BENCHMARKS

GRADE 2
- Present facts and simple answers to questions.
- Use simple rubrics to assess work.
- Reflect at the end of an inquiry experience about new ideas to wonder about and investigate.

GRADE 5
- Present information clearly so that main points are evident.
- Use information appropriate to task and audience.
- Identify and evaluate the important features for a good product.
- Identify their own strengths and set goals for improvement.
- Reflect at the end of an inquiry experience about what ideas would still be interesting to pursue.

GRADE 8
- Present conclusions and supporting facts in a variety of ways.
- Present solutions to problems using modeled examples.
- Identify, with guidance, skills that require practice and refinement.
- Follow plan of work but seek feedback for improving the process.
- Reflect at the end of an inquiry process to identify additional areas of personal interest for pursuit in the future.

GRADE 10
- Present and support conclusions to answer the question or problem.
- Set high and clear standards for work and develop criteria for self-assessment or use established criteria (rubrics, checklists).
- Assess their own work and establish revision strategies for themselves.
- Follow their own research plans and evaluate effectiveness of their inquiry processes.

GRADE 12
- Present complex ideas with clarity and authority.
- Present original conclusions effectively.
- Identify their own strengths, assess their own inquiry processes and products, and set goals for improvement.

INDICATOR 3.1.2:
Participate and collaborate as members of a social and intellectual network of learners.

GRADE-LEVEL BENCHMARKS

GRADE 2
- Participate in discussions and listen well.
- Show respect for the ideas of others.
- Give positive feedback.
- Respect rules and procedures as responsible library users.
- Share favorite literature, both fiction and nonfiction.

(continues on page 30)

(continued from page 29)

– Begin to create collaborative projects.

– Share information and creative products with others, using diverse formats, both print and nonprint.

GRADE 5	– Show respect for and respond to ideas of others.
	– Accurately describe or restate ideas of others.
	– Acknowledge personal and group achievements.
	– Rely on feedback to improve product and process.
	– Respect the guidelines for responsible and ethical use of information resources.
	– Share favorite literature.
	– Participate in discussions on fiction and nonfiction related to curriculum.
	– Develop a product with peers and share with others.
	– Develop projects with peers that can be shared electronically and can challenge other students to answer questions or give opinions adding to the content (for example, shared book reviews, shared slide presentations).
GRADE 8	– Offer information and opinions at appropriate times in group discussions.
	– Encourage team members to share ideas and opinions.
	– Ask questions of others in a group to elicit their information and opinions.
	– Accurately describe or summarize ideas of others.
	– Practice responsible and ethical use of information resources, both in their own library and in other institutions.
	– Share reading experiences and favorite literature to build a relationship with others.
	– Use interactive tools to exchange data collected, collaborate to design products or solve problems, and learn curricular.
GRADE 10	– Seek ideas and opinions from others.
	– Respect and help groups find and incorporate diverse ideas.
	– Accurately describe or summarize ideas of others and respond appropriately.
	– Respect guidelines and comply with policies for access in different information environments (public libraries, museums, cultural institutions, agencies).
	– Recognize that equitable access to information depends on student responsibility.
	– Use interactive tools and websites to collaboratively design products and solve problems with peers, experts, and other audiences.
	– Share research and creative products with others.
GRADE 12	– Offer and defend information brought to group.
	– Seek consensus from a group, when appropriate, to achieve a stronger product.
	– Help to organize and integrate contributions of all group members into products.
	– Use technology tools to collaborate, publish, and interact with peers, experts, and other real-world audiences.

INDICATOR 3.1.3:

Use writing and speaking skills to communicate new understandings effectively.

GRADE-LEVEL BENCHMARKS

GRADE 2
- Choose and maintain a focus in a piece of writing.
- Add details from personal experience and research to support ideas.
- Use a variety of ways (through art, music, movement, and oral and written language) to present information and main ideas; use oral and written language in a variety of formats (for example, narrative text, poetry, podcasts).

GRADE 5
- Use significant details and relevant information to develop meaning.
- Present information coherently in oral, written, and visual sequence.
- Use clear and appropriate vocabulary to convey the intended message.
- Speak clearly to convey meaning.

GRADE 8
- Present conclusions so that main ideas are clearly stated and supported by evidence.
- Use relevant ideas and details to show insight into people, events, new knowledge, and personal background.
- Use dramatic, audio, and video presentation as appropriate for subject and audience.
- Adjust pacing, volume, and intonation appropriate to content and purpose.

GRADE 10
- Use an organizational structure that effectively connects ideas and creates the desired intent.
- Use the most appropriate format, tone, and language to communicate ideas and points of view clearly to different audiences.

GRADE 12
- Employ organizational and presentation structures (for example, narrative essays, poems, debates) using various formats to achieve purpose and clarify meaning.
- Use details and language that shows authority and knowledge of topic.
- Deliver a presentation to support a position on a specified topic and respond to questions from the audience.
- Present ideas and conclusions to audiences beyond the school.

INDICATOR 3.1.4:

Use technology and other information tools to organize and display knowledge and understanding in ways that others can view, use, and assess.

GRADE-LEVEL BENCHMARKS

GRADE 2
- Use word processing and drawing tools to organize and communicate ideas.

GRADE 5
- Use various technology tools to retrieve and organize information.
- Use a variety of media and formats to create and edit products that communicate syntheses of information and ideas.

GRADE 8
- Use appropriate media and formats to design and develop products that clearly and coherently display new understanding.

GRADE 10
- Use a variety of media and formats to communicate information and ideas effectively to multiple audiences.

GRADE 12
- Prepare and deliver a "professional" presentation to audiences outside of school using technology as medium of presentation.

INDICATOR 3.1.5:

Connect learning to community issues.

GRADE-LEVEL BENCHMARKS

GRADE 2
– Express personal connections to the topic or question.
– Identify how the topic or question relates to a real-world need.

GRADE 5
– Gather ideas and information from different points of view.
– Base opinions on information from multiple sources of authority.
– Examine the concept of freedom of speech and explain why it is important.
– Connect ideas and information to situations and people in the larger community.

GRADE 8
– Identify and address community and global issues.
– Use real-world examples to establish authenticity.
– Seek information from different sources to get balanced points of view.
– Articulate the importance of intellectual freedom to a democratic society.

GRADE 10
– Use multiple resources to seek balanced perspectives.
– Explain how the topic or question relates to issues in the real world.
– Demonstrate understanding of intellectual freedom and First Amendment rights.

GRADE 12
– Investigate multiple sides of issues and evaluate them carefully, particularly on controversial or culturally based topics.
– Connect learning to real-world issues.

INDICATOR 3.1.6:

Use information and technology ethically and responsibly.

GRADE-LEVEL BENCHMARKS

GRADE 2
– Rephrase rather than copy whole sentences.
– Credit sources by citing author and title.
– Distinguish between acceptable and unacceptable computer use.
– Follow school guidelines related to the acceptable use of technology.
– Use technology in appropriate ways outside the school.

GRADE 5
– Demonstrate understanding of plagiarism by paraphrasing information or noting direct quotes.
– Understand that authors and illustrators own their writings and art, and it is against the law to copy their work.
– Credit all sources properly with title, author, and page number.
– Observe Web safety procedures including safeguarding personal information.
– Practice responsible use of technology and describe personal consequences of inappropriate use.
– Respect privacy of others (e-mail, files, passwords, book checkout, etc.).

GRADE 8
– Avoid plagiarism by rephrasing information in their own words.
– Document quotations and cite sources using correct bibliographic format.
– Abide by Acceptable Use Policy by accessing only appropriate information.
– Use programs and websites responsibly and ethically.

GRADE 10
- Understand what constitutes plagiarism and refrain from representing others' work as their own.
- Demonstrate understanding of intellectual property rights by giving credit for all quotes, and by citing them properly in notes and bibliography.
- Abide by copyright guidelines for use of materials not in public domain.
- Legally obtain, store, and disseminate text, data, images, or sounds.
- Abide by the Acceptable Use Policy in all respects and use Internet responsibly and safely.
- Explain First Amendment rights and the process available to defend them.

GRADE 12
- Demonstrate understanding for the process of copyrighting their own work.
- Analyze the consequences and costs of unethical use of information and communication technology (for example, hacking, spamming, consumer fraud, virus setting, intrusion); identify ways of addressing those risks.
- Use programs and websites responsibly, efficiently, and ethically.
- Serve as a mentor for others who want to use information technology.

STANDARD 4: Pursue personal and aesthetic growth.

STRAND 4.1: SKILLS

INDICATOR 4.1.1:
Read, view, and listen for pleasure and personal growth.

GRADE-LEVEL BENCHMARKS

GRADE 2
- Distinguish between what is real and what is not real.
- Request and choose materials related to personal interests.
- Read, view, and listen to a variety of fiction and nonfiction for enjoyment and information.
- Begin to recognize that different genres require different reading, listening, or viewing strategies.

GRADE 5
- Set reading goals.
- Read, listen to, and view a range of resources for a variety of purposes: to live the experiences of a character, to answer questions, to find out about something new, to explore personal interests.
- Visit the public library to attend programs, seek help as needed, and check out materials to read.

GRADE 8
- Read, listen to, and view an increasingly wide range of genres and formats for recreation and information.
- Independently locate and select information for personal, hobby, or vocational interests.
- Pursue creative expressions of information in the community (public library, arts centers, museums).

(continues on page 34)

(continued from page 33)

GRADE 10
- Read, listen to, and view information in a variety of formats to explore new ideas, form opinions, and solve problems.
- Seek and locate information about personal interests, applying the same criteria and strategies used for academic information seeking.

GRADE 12
- Read, view, and listen to learn, to solve problems, and to explore many different ideas.
- Routinely read, view, and listen for personal enjoyment.
- For personal growth and learning take advantage of opportunities available within the community, including classes, lectures, author presentations, museums, public library programming, and arts performances.

INDICATOR 4.1.2:

Read widely and fluently to make connections with self, the world, and previous reading.

GRADE-LEVEL BENCHMARKS

GRADE 2
- Read widely from multicultural texts in various genres to find out about self and the surrounding world.
- Predict what will happen next in a story.
- Draw conclusions about main idea of a story.
- Identify author's purpose and connect illustrations to a story.
- Compare and contrast characters in two different stories or plots in two stories by the same author.
- Retell a story using their own words and pictures.

GRADE 5
- Use evidence from the text to discuss the author's purpose.
- Read widely to explore new ideas.
- Predict and infer about events and characters.
- Identify problems and solutions in a story.
- Draw conclusions about the theme of a story.
- Describe how an illustrator's style and use of elements and media represent and extend the meaning of the story or the narrative text.
- Connect story to previous reading.
- Recognize features of various genres and use different reading strategies for understanding.
- Demonstrate knowledge of favorite authors and genres.

GRADE 8
- Read books that connect to their own experiences.
- Read with purpose to investigate new ideas beyond the required curriculum.
- Read books from various genres.
- Compare and contrast story elements in two literary works.
- Demonstrate understanding that texts, both narrative and expository, are written by authors expressing their own ideas.
- Recognize the author's point of view; consider alternative perspectives.

GRADE 10
- Recognize and evaluate the author's point of view and how it affects the text; consider and evaluate alternative perspectives.
- Read books that connect to real-world issues.
- Recognize similarities and differences among authors writing on the same theme.
- Recognize how their own points of view influence perspectives on text.

GRADE 12
- Read, view, and use fiction and nonfiction to enrich understanding of real-world concepts.
- Derive multiple perspectives on the same themes by comparing across different works.
- Read widely to develop a global perspective and understand different cultural contexts.
- Read to support and challenge their own points of view.

INDICATOR 4.1.3:
Respond to literature and creative expressions of ideas in various formats and genres.

GRADE-LEVEL BENCHMARKS

GRADE 2
- Express feelings about characters and events in a story.
- Make connections between literature and their own experiences.
- Write about or orally share reactions to imaginative stories and performances.
- Retell stories using the correct sequence of events.
- Identify plot, characters, times, and places in a story.
- Discuss favorite books and authors.

GRADE 5
- Connect their own feelings to emotions, characters, and events portrayed in a literary work.
- Use personal experiences to stimulate responses to literature and art.
- Restate and interpret ideas presented through creative formats.
- Identify story elements in various fiction genres.
- Use evidence from stories to discuss characters, setting, plot, time, and place.
- Discuss theme of stories, using evidence to support opinions.
- Participate in book talks and book discussion groups.

GRADE 8
- Respond to the images and feelings evoked by a literary or artistic work.
- Connect text to personal experiences.
- Use illustrations, context, graphics, and layout to extract meaning from different formats.
- Interpret literary elements (plot, setting, characters, time) from evidence presented in the text.
- Draw conclusions about the theme from evidence in the text.
- Recognize how characters change.
- Share reading, listening, and viewing experiences in a variety of ways and formats.

(continues on page 36)

(continued from page 35)

GRADE 10
– Assess the emotional impact of specific works on the reader or viewer.

– Apply ideas gained from literary and artistic works to their own lives.

– Compare the theme and its treatment in different works of literature.

– Evaluate the effectiveness of a creative work in terms of the creator's use and interweaving of artistic elements.

GRADE 12
– Express new ideas gained through information presented in various formats and connect the ideas to the human experience.

– Identify universal themes in literature and other creative forms of expression and analyze different cultural approaches to those themes.

INDICATOR 4.1.4:

Seek information for personal learning in a variety of formats and genres.

GRADE-LEVEL BENCHMARKS

GRADE 2
– Routinely select picture, fiction, and information books; try some books in other genres (poetry, fairy tales).

– Select information in various formats and genres based on suggestions from teacher or SLMS and on personal interests.

– Select some books at the appropriate reading level, other books to be read aloud, and other more challenging books of particular interest for browsing and enjoyment.

– Explain personal criteria for selecting a particular resource.

GRADE 5
– Select books from favorite authors and genres; try new genres when suggested.

– Select information in various formats based on a theme, topic, and connection to classroom learning or personal interest.

– Routinely select both "just right" books and challenging books.

– Read the multiple works of a single author.

– Explain why some authors and genres have become favorites.

– Independently select appropriate print, nonprint, and electronic materials on an individual level.

GRADE 8
– Read a variety of genres, including short stories, novels, poems, plays, drama, myths, films, and electronic magazines and books.

– Describe the characteristics of different genres.

– Explore new genres that fulfill interests and reading level (graphic novels, magazines, online magazines, e-books).

– Select resources for classroom learning and for personal exploration.

– Select resources on topics of interest at both a comfortable reading level and at higher levels of comprehension.

– Select print, nonprint, and electronic materials based on personal interests and knowledge of authors.

– Maintain personal reading lists.

GRADE 10
– Select resources for academic, personal, and real-world purposes.

– Select print, nonprint, and digital materials based on personal interests and knowledge of authors.

- Select resources on topics of interest at both comfortable and challenging levels of comprehension.

- Read a variety of fiction and nonfiction, including works of international authors and authors outside students' own cultures.

- Use print, nonprint, and electronic information resources for information about personal needs; actively seek answers to questions.

- Set reading goals and maintain personal reading lists.

GRADE 12	– Explore real-world genres (movie reviews, editorials, consumer reports, game tips and strategies, career information). – Find information about personal interests independently, using the same criteria and strategies used to seek academic information.

INDICATOR 4.1.5: Connect ideas to own interests and previous knowledge and experience.	**GRADE-LEVEL BENCHMARKS**
GRADE 2	– Prior to reading a book, gain background knowledge about the author or subject by discussing it with friend, teacher, or parent. – Demonstrate comprehension of stories read independently or shared aloud. – Develop criteria for deciding if a book matches interests and reading levels. – Find and read (or be read) books that match interests and comprehension levels.
GRADE 5	– Use prior knowledge to understand and compare literature. – Understand literal meaning and identify the main points reflected in a work. – Compare the ideas in various types of resources to experiences in real life.
GRADE 8	– Demonstrate understanding of literal and implied meanings by explaining how new meanings fit with what is already known. – Connect ideas reflected in various resources to life experiences at home, in school, and with peers. – Keep logs or records of new and up-to-date ideas by reading online information, magazines, and other current sources. – Check ideas for accuracy by analyzing the authority of the source and validating the information through multiple resources.
GRADE 10	– Explain text on both literal and abstract levels. – Use context and graphic clues to aid understanding. – Analyze alternative perspectives and evaluate differing points of view. – Compare new ideas to previous understandings and make changes to mental framework where appropriate.
GRADE 12	– Connect new ideas and understandings to future needs and interests that relate to college, careers, and personal lives. – Reflect on changes in personal goals, reading preferences, personal interests, and knowledge base throughout the high school experience.

INDICATOR 4.1.6:

Organize personal knowledge in a way that can be called upon easily.

GRADE-LEVEL BENCHMARKS

GRADE 2
– Take notes using graphic organizer provided by teacher or SLMS.
– Draw pictures of main ideas.

GRADE 5
– Use simple graphic organizers and technology tools to capture the main ideas and their relationships to each other.
– Use two-column approach to note-taking to capture personal connections to information.

GRADE 8
– Develop visual pictures of the main ideas and design concept maps, webs, or graphics to capture the ideas.
– Identify their own learning styles and organize ideas accordingly (for example, linear, graphic).
– Use different forms of note-taking to capture personal connections to information.

GRADE 10
– Use visualization to provide a clear picture of the major ideas.
– Categorize new ideas with keywords and tagging.
– Develop personal note-taking systems that incorporate personal reflections.

GRADE 12
– Connect new information to ideas previously learned by developing graphic organizers and taxonomies (hierarchical classifications) to link large concepts to related details.
– Identify the main ideas by seeing the pattern they present (for example, cause and effect, growth or change over time).
– Standardize personal note-taking systems so that main ideas and personal responses (emotional reactions, questions) are incorporated.

INDICATOR 4.1.7:

Use social networks and information tools to gather and share information.

GRADE-LEVEL BENCHMARKS

GRADE 2
– Locate information for personal interests and school assignments in print, nonprint, and electronic sources with guidance from the SLMS.
– Experiment with online catalog and Web resources to locate information.

GRADE 5
– Use basic strategies (author, title, subject) to locate information using the library's online catalog.
– Use social networking tools to create and share information.

GRADE 8
– Use advanced strategies (Boolean searches) to locate information about personal-interest topics in the library's online catalog.
– Use a few technology tools and resources to collect, organize, and evaluate information that addresses issues or interests.
– Apply technology productivity tools to meet personal needs.
– Use social networking tools to responsibly and safely share information and ideas and to collaborate with others.

GRADE 10
– Expand use of technology tools and resources to collect, organize, and evaluate information that addresses issues or interests.

- Use a range of search strategies to locate information about personal-interest topics in their own and other libraries.

- Engage in safe and ethical use of social networking applications to construct and share ideas and products.

- Share reading, viewing, and listening experiences in a variety of ways and formats, including book clubs and interest groups.

GRADE 12
- Address real-world problems and issues by using information and communication technology tools to gather, evaluate, and use information from different sources, analyze findings, draw conclusions, and create solutions.

- Use telecommunication to search for and identify potential work, college, or other opportunities.

- Apply production strategies and technology tools to design products to meet personal needs.

- Participate in the social interchange of ideas through book discussions, interest groups, and online sharing.

- Participate responsibly and safely in social networks using appropriate tools to collaborate, as well as to share ideas and knowledge.

INDICATOR 4.1.8:
Use creative and artistic formats to express personal learning.

GRADE-LEVEL BENCHMARKS

GRADE 2
- Express feelings about a story through pictures and words.
- Use technology tools to create and present ideas.
- Express their own ideas through simple products in different formats.

GRADE 5
- Present creative products in a variety of formats.
- Use technology applications to create documents and visualizations of new learning.
- Use multimedia authoring tools for independent and collaborative publishing activities.

GRADE 8
- Create original products based on responses to literature and other creative works of art.
- Experiment with various types of multimedia applications for artistic and personal expression.

GRADE 10
- Express their own ideas through creative products in a variety of formats.
- Choose format appropriate for audience and purpose.
- Select and use various types of multimedia applications for artistic and personal expression.

GRADE 12
- Create original products to reflect personal interpretations of information and construction of new knowledge using multiple formats.
- Use a range of technology tools to produce sophisticated and creative renditions of personal learning.

3 DISPOSITIONS IN ACTION

Defining Dispositions in 21st-Century Learning

One of the core functions of 21st-century education is learning to learn in preparation for a lifetime of change (Claxton 2007). Acquiring knowledge alone does not guarantee that this learning will be used and applied. Learning in the twenty-first century also requires a capacity to learn that reflects a range of dispositions: to be curious, resilient, flexible, imaginative, critical, reflective, and self-evaluative (Costa and Kallick 2000, Perkins 1992).

Dispositions have been variously described as habits of mind, attitudes, and learning behaviors. Regardless of the term used, a disposition is a tendency to exhibit frequently, consciously, and voluntarily a pattern of behavior that is directed to a broad goal (Katz 2000). Dispositions are not defined simply by the acquisition of skills. One can be proficient in a particular skill

without intentionally and mindfully using it. In other words, *having* is not the same as *doing*. For example, students may know how to evaluate websites, but if they do not believe that evaluation is critical, they revert to mindlessly selecting the first websites in their Google searches. Importantly, dispositions are not inborn. They can be supported and strengthened with curriculum and teaching strategies. Instructors foster desirable dispositions by challenging students to consider not only *what* they are learning, but also *how* they are learning and *why* they value the learning.

Dispositions and the Learning Process

Dispositions can be displayed at any point in the learning process. They are neither standard-specific, nor grade-level-specific. For example, persistence can be demonstrated at all grade levels by pursuing information to gain a broad perspective (Standard 1), positing a conclusion and testing it against the evidence (Standard 2), contributing responsibly in learning situations (Standard 3), and seeking information that answers personal questions and interests (Standard 4).

Teaching for Dispositions

Dispositions are developed over time by the way that educators structure learning experiences. For example, if SLMSs and classroom teachers give students quick assignments where they are expected to grasp whatever information they can find quickly, then they will not have opportunities to demonstrate persistence. If SLMSs and classroom teachers do not value multiple perspectives as evidenced by the way they structure and grade assignments, then students will not persist in finding a broad perspective.

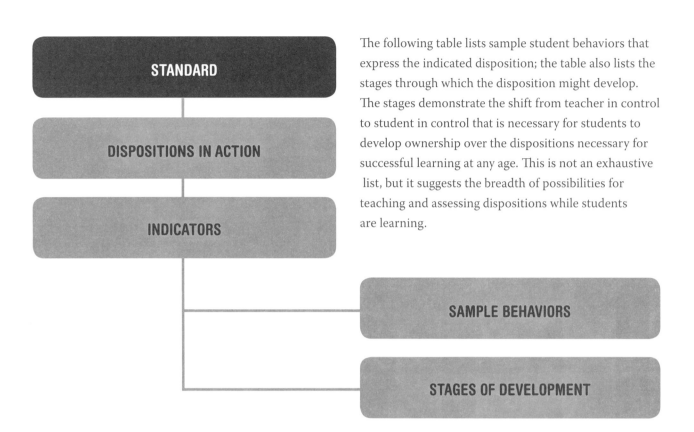

The following table lists sample student behaviors that express the indicated disposition; the table also lists the stages through which the disposition might develop. The stages demonstrate the shift from teacher in control to student in control that is necessary for students to develop ownership over the dispositions necessary for successful learning at any age. This is not an exhaustive list, but it suggests the breadth of possibilities for teaching and assessing dispositions while students are learning.

STANDARD 1: Inquire, think critically, and gain knowledge.

INDICATOR 1.2.1:
Display initiative and engagement by posing questions and investigating the answers beyond the collection of superficial facts.

SAMPLE BEHAVIORS

– Develop questions that relate to the essential or overarching question in the inquiry.
– Develop questions that explore the larger topic or issue to gain essential background knowledge.
– Develop questions that focus on "How do we know what we know?"
– Develop questions that require making connections between ideas and events.
– Develop questions that challenge previous thinking.

STAGES OF DEVELOPMENT

STAGE 1 – Pose questions but largely at the factual level.

STAGE 2 – Pose questions at both the factual and higher levels of thinking with considerable guidance from the teacher or SLMS.

STAGE 3 – Pose questions at both the factual and higher levels of thinking with minimal assistance from the teacher or SLMS.

INDICATOR 1.2.2:
Demonstrate confidence and self-direction by making independent choices in the selection of resources and information.

SAMPLE BEHAVIORS

– Preview resources to decide which best meet information needs.
– Apply evaluation strategies and criteria to select resources.
– Revise searches based on information found.

STAGES OF DEVELOPMENT

STAGE 1 – Seek continual assistance from teacher, SLMS, and peers in selecting resources and information.

STAGE 2 – Use strategies and criteria provided by the teacher or SLMS to select appropriate resources.

STAGE 3 – Work independently in evaluating resources and information and in revising search strategies as needed.

INDICATOR 1.2.3:
Demonstrate creativity by using multiple resources and formats.

SAMPLE BEHAVIORS

– Collect needed information from resources in a range of formats.
– Experiment with new ways to communicate information.

STAGES OF DEVELOPMENT

STAGE 1 – Use the same types of resources and formats for all information needs.

STAGE 2 – Use an expanding range of resources and formats that have been suggested by the teacher or SLMS.

STAGE 3 – Use a range of resources and formats, and try different ways to appropriately present information.

INDICATOR 1.2.4:

Maintain a critical stance by questioning the validity and accuracy of all information.

SAMPLE BEHAVIORS

– Distinguish fact from opinion.
– Detect bias.
– Use additional sources to verify conflicting information.

STAGES OF DEVELOPMENT

STAGE 1 – Tend to accept all information at face value.

STAGE 2 – Examine the soundness and relevance of information with considerable teacher or SLMS guidance and prompting.

STAGE 3 – Critically examine the soundness and relevance of information as an integral aspect of any learning process with little prompting from teacher or SLMS.

INDICATOR 1.2.5:

Demonstrate adaptability by changing the inquiry focus, questions, resources, or strategies when necessary to achieve success.

SAMPLE BEHAVIORS

– Modify inquiry focus based on data collected.
– Revise questions based on new information.
– Modify search strategies to deal with emerging findings.

STAGES OF DEVELOPMENT

STAGE 1 – Tend to stick with original focuses and questions, even when information gathered indicates a need for adjustments.

STAGE 2 – Make changes to the original focuses and questions based on data collected, but need considerable help in identifying new resources and adapting strategies to move ahead.

STAGE 3 – Require limited assistance to modify research focuses, questions, and search strategies; independently select additional resources as needed.

INDICATOR 1.2.6:

Display emotional resilience by persisting in information searching despite challenges.

SAMPLE BEHAVIORS

– Brainstorm new ways of searching for information when the existing strategy does not work.
– Analyze challenges faced in the research process and identify the possible barriers.

STAGES OF DEVELOPMENT

STAGE 1 – Need continual encouragement when first attempts to find information are not successful.

STAGE 2 – With occasional help and emotional support from the teacher or SLMS, identify alternative strategies to find needed information.

STAGE 3 – Reflect on why original search strategies did not work; independently determine additional possibilities.

INDICATOR 1.2.7:

Display persistence by continuing to pursue information to gain a broad perspective.

SAMPLE BEHAVIORS

– Use ranges of resources to search for broader or deeper perspectives on inquiries.
– Display continuing curiosity that fuels self-generated investigation of inquiries.

STAGES OF DEVELOPMENT

STAGE 1	– Limit information pursuits to the requirements of assignments.
STAGE 2	– Generate additional questions and use additional resources that demonstrate more depth than required by the original assignments.
STAGE 3	– Show evidence of pursuing questions even after the original assignments have been completed.

STANDARD 2: Draw conclusions, make informed decisions, apply knowledge to new situations, and create new knowledge.

INDICATOR 2.2.1:

Demonstrate flexibility in the use of resources by adapting information strategies to each specific resource and by seeking additional resources when clear conclusions cannot be drawn.

SAMPLE BEHAVIORS

– Realize that Web searching and book searching require different skills and adapt accordingly.
– Detect conflicting information and access resources that contribute to thoughtful conclusions.

STAGES OF DEVELOPMENT

STAGE 1	– Use the same strategies for searching regardless of the format or medium and the appropriateness and comprehensiveness of the information for drawing a conclusion.
STAGE 2	– Adjust search strategies depending on the format or medium being used, but tend not to resolve conflicting or unclear findings.
STAGE 3	– Detect conflicting information and retrieve data to resolve or clarify findings; independently adapt search techniques to locate necessary information in different formats.

INDICATOR 2.2.2:

Use both divergent and convergent thinking to formulate alternative conclusions and test them against the evidence.

SAMPLE BEHAVIORS

– Explore a wide range of possible conclusions and analyze the evidence to support them.
– Bring together information to solve a problem or reach a conclusion.

STAGES OF DEVELOPMENT

STAGE 1	– Identify one possible conclusion but require considerable guidance from the teacher or SLMS to come up with other possibilities.
STAGE 2	– Identify more than one possible conclusion but require considerable guidance from the teacher or SLMS while devising ways to determine which conclusions can actually be supported.
STAGE 3	– Identify a range of possible conclusions and determine techniques to test them against the evidence while requiring limited help from the teacher or SLMS.

INDICATOR 2.2.3:

Employ a critical stance in drawing conclusions by demonstrating that the pattern of evidence leads to a decision or conclusion.

SAMPLE BEHAVIORS

- Recognize fallacies in logic.
- Identify misleading information and gaps in information that lead to inaccurate conclusions.
- Read widely from varied sources to pinpoint inaccurate information.

STAGES OF DEVELOPMENT

STAGE 1	– Draw questionable conclusions based on shallow or incomplete evidence.
STAGE 2	– Draw plausible conclusions but need help from the teacher or SLMS to articulate how the evidence supports those conclusions.
STAGE 3	– Draw conclusions or make decisions based on clearly documented evidence drawn from a range of appropriate resources.

INDICATOR 2.2.4:

Demonstrate personal productivity by completing products to express learning.

SAMPLE BEHAVIORS

- Establish a research plan that outlines learning goals, identifies major tasks and deadlines to achieve steps toward the goals, and documents progress throughout the research process.
- Set and meet high standards and goals for delivering quality work on time.

STAGES OF DEVELOPMENT

STAGE 1	– With considerable help from the teacher or SLMS, develop a simple plan (goals, tasks, deadlines) for conducting research.
STAGE 2	– Develop a detailed plan (goals, tasks, criteria to assess work, deadlines) but need periodic reminders from the teacher or SLMS to complete the work in a timely manner.
STAGE 3	– Develop a detailed plan and self-monitor progress in completing high-quality work in a timely manner.

STANDARD 3: Share knowledge and participate ethically and productively as members of our democratic society.

INDICATOR 3.2.1:

Demonstrate leadership and confidence by presenting ideas to others in both formal and informal situations.

SAMPLE BEHAVIORS

- Present findings of an inquiry project in an organized, articulate, and poised delivery.
- In small group and large group settings freely communicate ideas and opinions that are thoughtfully supported.

STAGES OF DEVELOPMENT

STAGE 1	– Share ideas and opinions comfortably in informal settings.
STAGE 2	– Share ideas and opinions comfortably in both informal and formal settings.
STAGE 3	– Frequently facilitate exchange of ideas and opinions in informal settings; share ideas with poise and confidence in formal situations.

INDICATOR 3.2.2:

Show social responsibility by participating actively with others in learning situations and by contributing questions and ideas during group discussions.

SAMPLE BEHAVIORS

– Listen respectfully and objectively; offer constructive feedback.
– Contribute opinions, ideas, and questions in a responsible manner.

STAGES OF DEVELOPMENT

STAGE 1	– Listen respectfully but rarely contribute to the group discussions.
STAGE 2	– Listen respectfully and when appropriate, offer information and opinions in group discussions.
STAGE 3	– Listen respectfully, contribute and ask clarifying questions, and often take the lead in encouraging others to share their ideas and opinions.

INDICATOR 3.2.3:

Demonstrate teamwork by working productively with others.

SAMPLE BEHAVIORS

– Take on different roles and tasks willingly within the group to accomplish shared ends.
– Help to leverage strengths of others to accomplish a common goal.
– Use problem-solving skills to influence and guide others toward a goal.

STAGES OF DEVELOPMENT

STAGE 1	– Seldom volunteer but will complete tasks assigned by the team.
STAGE 2	– Assume different roles in a team to complete tasks and achieve goals.
STAGE 3	– Frequently assume leadership in the team; seek consensus to achieve goals.

STANDARD 4: Pursue personal and aesthetic growth.

INDICATOR 4.2.1:

Display curiosity by pursuing interests through multiple resources.

SAMPLE BEHAVIORS

– Explore print, digital, and other resources to find information on a topic of personal interest.
– Seek diverse opinions and points of view while critically investigating a topic of personal interest.

STAGES OF DEVELOPMENT

STAGE 1	– Satisfy personal information needs using the same limited resources.
STAGE 2	– Satisfy personal information needs using new (to the students) as well as familiar resources in a range of formats.
STAGE 3	– Satisfy personal information needs using a range of information sources; demonstrate evidence of seeking different views and opinions on these topics.

INDICATOR 4.2.2:

Demonstrate motivation by seeking information to answer personal questions and interests, trying a variety of formats and genres, and displaying a willingness to go beyond academic requirements.

SAMPLE BEHAVIORS

– Voluntarily generate questions that go beyond an assignment.
– Independently pursue answers to self-generated questions.

STAGES OF DEVELOPMENT

STAGE 1 – Show limited interest in reading, viewing, or listening to meet personal needs.

STAGE 2 – Explore a range of resources to answer personal questions and pursue personal interests.

STAGE 3 – Explore various information formats and literary genres to meet personal needs; voluntarily pursue questions generated by class assignments.

INDICATOR 4.2.3:

Maintain openness to new ideas by considering divergent opinions, changing opinions or conclusions when evidence supports the change, and seeking information about new ideas encountered through academic or personal experiences.

SAMPLE BEHAVIORS

– Willingly accept diverse points of views and ideas and carefully analyze them.
– Modify personal view or conclusion based on the analysis of new information and evidence.

STAGES OF DEVELOPMENT

STAGE 1 – Acknowledge opinions of other people on a particular topic or issue.

STAGE 2 – Consider documented evidence and other people's views on a particular topic or issue in developing personal opinions.

STAGE 3 – Develop personal views on a topic or issue by taking into account documented evidence and views expressed by others, and by pursuing additional and divergent information.

INDICATOR 4.2.4:

Show an appreciation for literature by electing to read for pleasure and expressing an interest in various literary genres.

SAMPLE BEHAVIORS

– Read as a voluntary, out-of-class pursuit.
– Select and enjoy a range of print and digital resources based on personal interests.
– Maintain personal reading lists.

STAGES OF DEVELOPMENT

STAGE 1 – Read when required; tend to stick with a preferred genre.

STAGE 2 – Read voluntarily for pleasure; independently explore various genres.

STAGE 3 – Read voluntarily for pleasure in a range of genres; maintain personal reading logs.

Defining Responsibilities in 21st-Century Learning

Learning in the twenty-first century requires active participation by the learner. A learned person is not one who has simply memorized theorems or passively accepted conclusions drawn by others. A learned person must take *responsibility* for actively pursuing information and ideas both in print and digitally, understanding those ideas and how they apply, drawing conclusions and developing new applications, and sharing these new understandings with others. Responsibilities, then, can be defined as the common behaviors that must be exhibited during researching, investigating, and problem solving to develop new understanding successfully, ethically, and thoughtfully. Responsibilities are key to successful learning in the twenty-first century.

The 21st-century context has led to an interesting blend between independent and social learning and, therefore, between individual and social responsibilities. The digital environment makes greater amounts of information available at learners' fingertips and at the time of need. As a result, learners experience pressure to be independent in their information searching because they often are using information tools when personal support from their teacher or SLMS is not available. At the same time, the tools of learning and the increasingly globalized context of society provide opportunities and obligations to collaborate, seek divergent perspectives, work effectively in groups, and share learning products and processes.

Therefore, during the learning process, learners have responsibilities to themselves and to others. For themselves, learners must follow ethical and legal guidelines, respect the principles of intellectual freedom, and pursue multiple perspectives and a balance of viewpoints before making decisions or drawing conclusions; practice safe behaviors in the use of social tools; seek opportunities for pursuing personal and aesthetic growth; and connect their learning to real-world issues and ideas. For others, learners have a responsibility to contribute to the exchange of ideas in a learning community, both electronically and in person; respect the ideas and experiences of others; and use information and knowledge in service of democratic values.

Responsibilities and the Learning Process

Responsibilities, like dispositions, can be displayed at any point in the learning process and are neither standard-specific, nor grade-level-specific. The same responsibilities may be necessary whether learners are investigating, drawing conclusions, sharing knowledge, or reading for enjoyment. For example, learners have a responsibility to their community of learners to contribute to the exchange of ideas. They might share book reviews on a wiki or participate in a book discussion group (Standard 4), or they might bring their individually researched evidence and conclusions to a group discussion to help the group reach a valid and ethical decision (Standard 2).

Teaching for Responsibilities

Responsibilities are developed when learning experiences are structured for active engagement and sharing. This requires a shift from pure didactic instruction (with the SLMS in control) to a more constructivist approach that combines direct instruction with opportunities for guided and independent practice (with empowered learners in control of their own learning). Responsibilities must be developed over time, with strong support initially and gradual reduction of guidance until students have assumed the responsibilities for themselves.

The following pages offer sample behaviors that indicate student performance of responsibility; the pages also list the stages through which the responsibility might develop. The stages demonstrate the shift from teacher in control to student in control that is necessary for students to develop ownership over the responsibilities necessary for successful learning at any age.

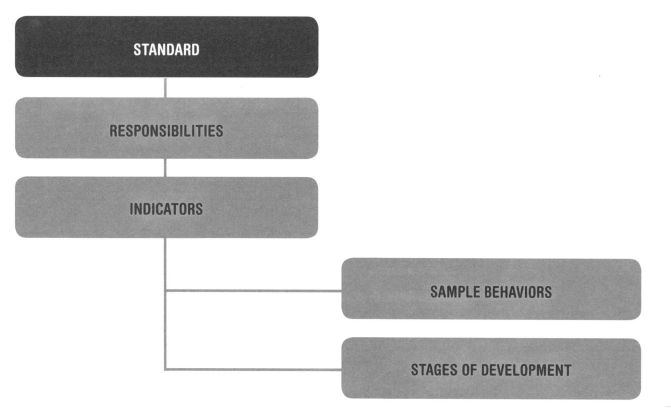

STANDARD 1: Inquire, think critically, and gain knowledge.

INDICATOR 1.3.1:
Respect copyright/intellectual property rights of creators and producers.

SAMPLE BEHAVIORS

– Cite the source for all information that is not commonly known or not in numerous sources.

– Use quotation marks for all material taken directly from a source.

– Put information into their own words rather than simply changing a word or two.

STAGES OF DEVELOPMENT

STAGE 1 – Acknowledge work of others by citing sources.

STAGE 2 – Provide reference citations for all direct quotations as well as cite sources.

STAGE 3 – Put information into their own words and provide credit, citations, and bibliography for all quoted and referenced information.

INDICATOR 1.3.2:
Seek divergent perspectives during information gathering and assessment.

SAMPLE BEHAVIORS

– Recognize when different perspectives exist about an issue.

– Seek credible sources that present different viewpoints.

– Evaluate every source to determine whether the author's point of view has skewed the accuracy of the information presented.

STAGES OF DEVELOPMENT

STAGE 1 – Find information to support one point of view, but acknowledge that another point of view exists.

STAGE 2 – Find information to represent two points of view about a research topic.

STAGE 3 – Find information that credibly represents all relevant perspectives on a research topic.

INDICATOR 1.3.3:
Follow ethical and legal guidelines in gathering and using information.

SAMPLE BEHAVIORS

– Follow copyright guidelines for text, visuals, and music in generating products and presentations.

– Present information accurately.

– Differentiate clearly between information gathered from sources and original thinking and conclusions.

STAGES OF DEVELOPMENT

STAGE 1 – Follow legal guidelines in using information using only excerpts and crediting the author or creator.

STAGE 2 – Follow copyright guidelines by using only excerpts and crediting the source of all text, visuals, and music, and follow ethical guidelines by presenting only accurate and valid information.

STAGE 3 – Gather and present information ethically by communicating an accurate, full, and unbiased picture of the topic and by clearly distinguishing between cited and original thinking.

INDICATOR 1.3.4:

Contribute to the exchange of ideas within the learning community.

SAMPLE BEHAVIORS

– Share relevant information to contribute to learning of others through discussions and presentations.

– Contribute opinions and supporting evidence to group deliberations.

– Listen to opinions and evidence of others.

– Ask and respond to questions in group exchanges of ideas.

STAGES OF DEVELOPMENT

STAGE 1	– Occasionally offer opinions and information to group discussions.
STAGE 2	– Whenever appropriate offer opinions with supporting evidence to group discussions.
STAGE 3	– Listen to opinions and evidence of others, and respond to them while offering their own opinion and evidence to group discussions.

INDICATOR 1.3.5:

Use information technology responsibly.

SAMPLE BEHAVIORS

– Purchase, rather than pirate, music and videos from the Web.

– Access only appropriate websites.

– Use digital social tools responsibly by protecting personal information and by posting only accurate and non-inflammatory information.

STAGES OF DEVELOPMENT

STAGE 1	– Use only digital tools and websites that have been pre-approved by teacher or SLMS.
STAGE 2	– Select and use appropriately digital tools and websites from choices presented by teacher or SLMS.
STAGE 3	– Use appropriate digital tools and websites independently in a safe and ethical manner (for example, appropriate to age and grade level, related to topic under consideration, authoritative information).

STANDARD 2: Draw conclusions, make informed decisions, apply knowledge to new situations, and create new knowledge.

INDICATOR 2.3.1:

Connect understanding to the real world.

SAMPLE BEHAVIORS

– Apply or adapt conclusions or decisions to new situations.
– Draw on understandings to make personal decisions.
– Make connections between real life and information gathered through research.

STAGES OF DEVELOPMENT

STAGE 1 – State in their own language what new understandings mean.

STAGE 2 – Apply knowledge to new situations.

STAGE 3 – Use what has been learned to make decisions or deal with situations in their personal lives.

INDICATOR 2.3.2:

Consider diverse and global perspectives in drawing conclusions.

SAMPLE BEHAVIORS

– Actively seek valid alternative perspectives when seeking information.
– Evaluate the authors and viewpoints of all information sources; use questions like:
  – Does this person or group have the knowledge and authority to represent this perspective?
  – Does the point of view influence the accuracy and reliability of the information?
– When appropriate seek sources written by authors in other parts of the world, rather than solely sources written by North American authors *about* other parts of the world.

STAGES OF DEVELOPMENT

STAGE 1 – Consider the point of view of the first source found in drawing conclusions.

STAGE 2 – Seek alternative perspectives before attempting to make decisions or draw conclusions.

STAGE 3 – Validate the authority and authenticity of diverse viewpoints before using the evidence to draw conclusions.

INDICATOR 2.3.3:

Use valid information and reasoned conclusions to make ethical decisions.

SAMPLE BEHAVIORS

– Use criteria to evaluate information before making decisions.
– Before reaching a decision consider all the evidence and the strength of support for conflicting views, rather than making a decision and then looking for evidence to support it.

STAGES OF DEVELOPMENT

STAGE 1 – Use information to make decisions.

STAGE 2 – Evaluate information before using it to make decisions.

STAGE 3 – Consider all relevant and accurate information before using it to make decisions.

STANDARD 3: Share knowledge and participate ethically and productively as members of our democratic society.

INDICATOR 3.3.1:

Solicit and respect diverse perspectives while searching for information, collaborating with others, and participating as a member of the community.

SAMPLE BEHAVIORS

– Solicit and listen respectfully to ideas and opinions of others.
– Build on the ideas of others in group conversations and discussions.
– State their own opinions respectfully, using evidence to back them up.
– Actively seek common ground in discussions where different viewpoints are expressed.
– Create safe zones where different viewpoints can be expressed without fear of disrespect or outright dismissal.

STAGES OF DEVELOPMENT

STAGE 1 – State their own opinions respectfully with evidence to back them up.

STAGE 2 – Listen to the opinions of others and modify their own opinions when appropriate.

STAGE 3 – Actively seek the opinions of others and create a group environment in which all participants' ideas are shared and valued.

INDICATOR 3.3.2:

Respect the differing interests and experiences of others, and seek a variety of viewpoints.

SAMPLE BEHAVIORS

– Recognize the benefits of differing viewpoints for expanding understanding.
– Ask leading questions that draw out the interests and experiences of others.

STAGES OF DEVELOPMENT

STAGE 1 – Recognize when people in a group have different opinions.

STAGE 2 – Track the changes of opinion that result from exposure to different ideas of others in the group.

STAGE 3 – Draw out and respond to the different interests and perspectives of members of a group.

INDICATOR 3.3.3:

Use knowledge and information skills and dispositions to engage in public conversation and debate around issues of common concern.

SAMPLE BEHAVIORS

– Engage with others in discussions and debates around important issues.
– Seek valid and accurate information on current issues to be able to contribute to group discussions.

STAGES OF DEVELOPMENT

STAGE 1 – Engage in conversations and debate by offering relevant information some of the time.

STAGE 2 – Engage in conversations and debate by offering relevant information often.

STAGE 3 – Engage in conversations and debate by offering relevant information most of the time.

INDICATOR 3.3.4:

Create products that apply to authentic, real-world contexts.

SAMPLE BEHAVIORS

– Produce ideas and projects that can be applied in real situations.

– Produce projects that connect with relevant issues in the local, national, and global communities.

STAGES OF DEVELOPMENT

STAGE 1 – Create products with real-world contexts that have been specified by the teacher or SLMS.

STAGE 2 – Create products that show the application of knowledge to real-world situations or issues.

STAGE 3 – Create products that have the quality and applicability to be used in the real world.

INDICATOR 3.3.5:

Contribute to the exchange of ideas within and beyond the learning community.

SAMPLE BEHAVIORS

– Participate actively as members of the learning community by contributing appropriate information, asking thoughtful questions, challenging questionable statements, and listening carefully to others.

– Move group idea exchanges to logical and inclusive conclusions by summarizing main points, finding consensus among ideas presented by different group members, and making sure that everyone in the group has had the opportunity to contribute.

– Present ideas publicly beyond the school learning community when opportunities become available.

STAGES OF DEVELOPMENT

STAGE 1 – Offer appropriate information to help groups deliberate and reach decisions together.

STAGE 2 – Question own and others' ideas to ensure that shared ideas are investigated thoroughly from all sides.

STAGE 3 – Challenge the thinking of groups to move them toward better decision making.

INDICATOR 3.3.6:

Use information and knowledge in the service of democratic values.

SAMPLE BEHAVIORS

– Make sure that all voices are heard within the learning community by encouraging participation, eliciting responses to questions, and inviting the expression of divergent opinions.

– Make sure that underrepresented viewpoints are heard and not stifled by the will of the majority.

– Bring groups to consensus of opinion.

– Seek justice and equity where research has shown they do not exist.

STAGES OF DEVELOPMENT

STAGE 1 – Encourage participation in sharing of information and decision-making by all members of school community.

STAGE 2 – Bring groups to consensus of opinion after all voices have been heard.

STAGE 3 – Apply group decision making to situations of larger democratic values, such as equity, freedom, and responsibility.

INDICATOR 3.3.7:

Respect the principles of intellectual freedom.

SAMPLE BEHAVIORS

- Exercise the right to express ideas freely and responsibly.
- Resist censorship of ideas and resources.
- Pursue the right to read, view, and listen.
- Ensure that one person's rights do not infringe on another's.

STAGES OF DEVELOPMENT

STAGE 1	– Exercise the right to express ideas freely and responsibly.
STAGE 2	– Actively preserve the rights of others to express ideas freely.
STAGE 3	– Ensure that one person's rights to speak or write freely do not infringe on the rights of others.

STANDARD 4: Pursue personal and aesthetic growth.

INDICATOR 4.3.1:

Participate in the social exchange of ideas, both electronically and in person.

SAMPLE BEHAVIORS

- Use social tools to communicate with and respond to others.
- Act responsibly and respectfully while communicating with others.

STAGES OF DEVELOPMENT

STAGE 1	– Use social tools occasionally to share information and communicate with others.
STAGE 2	– Use social tools often to share information and communicate with others.
STAGE 3	– Use social tools to share information and communicate with others as a normal part of daily academic and personal life.

INDICATOR 4.3.2:

Recognize that resources are created for a variety of purposes.

SAMPLE BEHAVIORS

- Identify reasons that different genres are created and choose appropriate genres for specific situations or interests.
- Recognize that the purpose of a resource influences its presentation and message.

STAGES OF DEVELOPMENT

STAGE 1	– Routinely read or view one or two different genres for personal enjoyment.
STAGE 2	– Read or view several different genres on a regular basis for personal enjoyment.
STAGE 3	– Read or view different genres on a regular basis that are selected because they match the personal reason for reading or viewing with the creator's purpose.

4. Responsibilities

INDICATOR 4.3.3:

Seek opportunities for pursuing personal and aesthetic growth.

SAMPLE BEHAVIORS

– Choose to read books for enjoyment.

– Find information to satisfy personal interests and questions.

– Express ideas and emotions through a variety of venues (artistic, written, oral).

STAGES OF DEVELOPMENT

STAGE 1	– Read occasionally for enjoyment and personal growth.
STAGE 2	– Read regularly for enjoyment and personal growth.
STAGE 3	– Read daily for enjoyment and personal growth.

INDICATOR 4.3.4:

Practice safe and ethical behaviors in personal electronic communication and interaction.

SAMPLE BEHAVIORS

– Restrict Web posting of personal information to remain within safety guidelines (no personally identifiable information).

– Maintain ethical standards in personal contributions to the Web (no bullying, slander, inflammatory language, or biased or inaccurate information).

– Refrain from downloading proprietary music, videos, or information without permission or purchase.

STAGES OF DEVELOPMENT

STAGE 1	– Maintain safe behavior when accessing websites for personal reasons.
STAGE 2	– Maintain safe behavior when accessing websites and refrain from downloading copyrighted material if it has not been purchased.
STAGE 3	– When accessing websites maintain safe and ethical behavior by protecting personal safety, displaying ethical and respectful behavior toward others, and following legal guidelines in downloading and use of material.

5 SELF-ASSESSMENT STRATEGIES

Defining Self-Assessment in 21st-Century Learning

Learners in the twenty-first century must take charge of their own learning to be able to sort through and make sense of the overwhelming amount of available information, and to use the information to fulfill personal and academic needs. Both the "what" and the "how" of learning have become so complex in today's global society that learners must make constant decisions throughout their own learning process. For example, they must ask themselves:

– "Do I have enough information to make a good decision?"

– "Am I getting good, unbiased information or is someone just trying to sell a point of view?"

– "Do I need to get the most current information online, and how do I make sure that information is accurate?"

These decisions are based on self-assessment, the cornerstone of independence in learning.

Self-assessment means developing internal standards and comparing performance, behaviors, or thoughts to those standards. A teacher or SLMS can assess the explicit products of students' learning processes (such as the number of ideas a student contributes to a group discussion or the effectiveness of a student's final presentation), but only the students can assess their own thinking, attitudes, and motivations. Self-assessment, then, involves a reflective process of self-monitoring according to internal standards ("How am I doing?") and metacognition ("How am I thinking?").

Self-Assessment and the Learning Process

At different points in the learning process learners may assess or reflect on their own processes of learning (skills, dispositions, responsibilities), their learning products (content, presentation), or their own thinking. Reflection must become intrinsic to learning so that learning is not defined as an accumulation of information, but rather as the thoughtful processing of information to produce, apply, and create knowledge. Self-assessment strategies are neither standard-specific, nor grade-level-specific.

Self-assessment is three-directional:

1) Looking backwards at work that has been done to see how successful it was (summative assessment).

2) Looking at the present to determine the next steps (formative assessment).

3) Looking at the future to decide what has been learned that will make the learning process more effective in the future (predictive assessment).

Self-assessment is enhanced by applying it in a social context because learning itself is social. Learners can assess their own performance and progress more effectively by:

- gathering feedback from others
- looking at how their individual skills contribute to group learning
- thinking about the responsibilities and dispositions that are most appropriate for the learning situation and others around them
- considering the applications of their learning to the real world.

Self-assessment with the opportunity to revise yields increased competence and confidence; that combination of competence and confidence leads to huge increases in achievement. The ultimate result of self-assessment is that students develop their own voices and become empowered to be independent and socially responsive learners.

Teaching for Self-Assessment

Students learn self-assessment through a combination of teaching strategies. **Direct instruction** is appropriate at any time, especially when students are learning a new self-assessment strategy, such as reflective note taking. SLMSs might, for example, teach students to ask themselves questions during note taking as they interact with text. ("Is this true?" "How does this fit with what I already know?" "Is there another viewpoint on this issue?" "What other questions do I have?") Rather than teaching specific strategies, SLMSs and teachers may choose to provide **models of exemplary performance** to enable students to internalize a solid understanding of the expectations and to compare their performance with the model. Finally, SLMSs and teachers may guide students' self-assessment by providing **scaffolding**.

When students are assessing their own learning, they may use strategies that involve reflection, feedback from others, or self-questioning. The following are examples of scaffolding that might be provided by the teacher or SLMS for each of these types of strategies. The examples are presented generically so that they can be adapted for any grade level or content area.

REFLECTION

Reflection Logs – Students routinely write in journals or logs about their research experience. They may indicate simply what they tried and what they accomplished each day, what frustrations or barriers they experienced, what they plan to do next, what questions they have about the subject or process, or what they want to remember later when creating their final product. SLMSs and teachers may scaffold attention to specific items or provoke continued progress by offering a prompt for the reflection-log writing. For example:

- "What was the most important idea you learned today?" and "Why is it the most important?"
- "What new question has emerged from your research, and how do you think you will find the answer?"
- "What's the best online source you've found?" and "Why is it the best?"

Although the SLMS or teacher will want to review and respond to the logs occasionally, their main value is to encourage the students' thinking about their own work.

Process Folios – Process folios are strategic collections of the process work of learning, just as portfolios are strategic collections of the products of learning. Students begin with a reflection on their whole research process, looking at the barriers and successes along the way. Students then document and reflect on the phases of their learning experience, which might include their initial topic selection, development of questions, search strategy, evaluation of sources, evaluation of information, reflective note taking, and organization of final product.

Reflective Note Taking – Many teachers and SLMSs teach students to make two- or three-column notes. This structure leads students to think about the notes while they are taking them because the right column is usually for student reactions to the ideas in the notes. SLMSs and teachers may provide prompts for the reflections column, or they may leave it up to students to react however they feel is appropriate. The result of using reflective note taking is that students have already made sense of the information before they try to draw conclusions, and to organize and create their final product.

USING FEEDBACK FROM OTHERS

Rubric or Checklist – Students may provide valuable feedback to their peers by using a rubric or checklist to look at the peers' work and providing comments for suggested revisions. Peer feedback is most useful in the skills area. Embedded within the latter part of this document are methods of assessing levels of proficiency for many of the 21st-century learning skills in these standards. These methods may easily be extracted and combined to provide a rubric for the skills being addressed during a particular learning experience.

Checklists offer a quicker way for peers to offer feedback. The items on the checklist should correspond with the skills being emphasized during that learning experience. The following chart is a brief example of a checklist for Standard 3: Share knowledge and participate ethically and productively as members of our democratic society.

Peer Questioning or Consultation – Students can help one another think through their learning processes by asking questions and engaging in conversations at strategic points. These peer-to-peer consultancies may be helpful at several phases during the process. Teachers and SLMSs may provide a set of questions for students to ask each other to help them structure the conversation. For example, at the early stages of research, students might ask:

- "What are the questions that you're trying to answer?"
- "Why do you want to know this?"
- "What do you already know?"
- "Where are you going to look to find the answers?"
- "What are the keywords that you think will help you search?"

SELF-QUESTIONING

Student self-assessment may be most effective when students learn to question themselves throughout the learning process. Teachers and SLMSs can scaffold self-questioning by providing questions that are specifically designed around the targeted skills, responsibilities, and dispositions for each learning experience. The following generic examples are provided for all four of the standards in *Standards for the 21st-Century Learner.*

Teachers and SLMSs may choose to invite students to participate in self-questioning by clearly communicating the value and purpose through a message similar to the sample provided.

STANDARD

SELF-ASSESSMENT STRATEGIES

INDICATORS

STUDENT SELF-QUESTIONING EXAMPLES

CRITERIA IN EVIDENCE	YES	PARTLY	NO
Outline or graphic organizer of ideas is reflected in the organization of the final product.			
Conclusion is clearly stated or presented.			
Evidence is offered that supports the conclusion.			
The format of the presentation is appropriate for the audience.			
All sources have been documented correctly.			
The final product shows clear understanding of the topic.			
The final product shows creativity.			

A MESSAGE TO THE STUDENT

As a student living and learning in the twenty-first century, your life is filled with accessibility and opportunities to interact with information and ideas in many formats. In school and at home you have many ways to retrieve information. As a learner you face many challenges. Electronic and print resources are very diverse and present information in a wide variety of formats. You must possess the skills for finding information and using that information appropriately and effectively. Your new understanding must be communicated to others using new tools and technologies. You live and work in a complex information landscape!

As you make your way toward a rapidly changing future, you are challenged to prepare yourself. As a 21st-century learner you are challenged to learn content, learn how to learn, and think about how well you are learning and performing. You participate in this process along with your teachers and other students. Reflecting on your learning and process is called "metacognition," meaning "thinking about thinking."

In taking charge of your learning you:

– define your problem or task

– investigate solutions

– evaluate and change your process

– make decisions about the effectiveness of your work

– evaluate the final outcome

The following questions can serve as a guide as you navigate the rapidly changing information landscape.

STANDARD 1: Inquire, think critically, and gain knowledge.

What interests me about this idea or topic?

Why am I doing this research?

How will I find out about this idea or topic?

What do I already know or think I know about this topic?

What background information would help me get an overview of my topic so that I can ask good questions and learn more about it?

What intriguing questions do I have about the topic or idea? Can my questions be answered through investigation?

What do I expect to find?

What is my plan for research?

What are all the sources that might be used?

Which sources will be most useful and valuable?

How do I locate these sources?

Have I located sources with diverse perspectives?

How do I find the information within each source?

How do I evaluate the information that I find?

Have I found enough accurate information to answer all my questions?

Have I discovered information gaps and filled them with more research?

Have I begun to identify relationships and patterns and thoughtfully reacted to the information I found?

Have any main ideas emerged from the research?

How well did my inquiry process go?

STANDARD 2: Draw conclusions, make informed decisions, apply knowledge to new situations, and create new knowledge.

How does the evidence I found help me form an opinion or support my thesis?

What organizational patterns will help me make sense of my information?

What technology tools will help me organize and make sense of my information?

What decisions or conclusions have I drawn, and how are they supported by the evidence?

What new understandings did I develop about the topic or idea?

How do those new understandings apply to other situations or contexts?

What did I learn about inquiry?

What new questions do I now want to answer about the topic or idea?

STANDARD 3: Share knowledge and participate ethically and productively as members of our democratic society.

What type of product or presentation will allow me to present my conclusions and evidence effectively to the intended audience?

How have I organized the product/presentation to make my major points and present convincing evidence?

What technology will help me create a product or presentation?

How will I get help to revise and edit my product?

How well does my product/presentation fulfill all the requirements of the assignment?

How can I make my product/presentation as effective as possible?

How can I get feedback on my final product to use in my next inquiry project?

How have I contributed to the learning of others?

How have I shown responsibility in finding and using information in an ethical way?

STANDARD 4: Pursue personal and aesthetic growth.

Why am I interested in this idea? How does it connect to what's important to me personally?

How can I find interesting information about this idea?

Why does this author or genre appeal to me? What other genres have I tried?

How can I make sense of information that is scattered among many different sources, both in print and online?

How does this compare to other things I've read or viewed?

Why did the author or creator produce this?

Does this work give me a slanted picture of the world?

How can I share this experience with others?

How can I use technology to communicate and interact with others?

How can I express my own ideas creatively and effectively?

6 BENCHMARKS AND ACTION EXAMPLES

The AASL *Standards for the 21st-Century Learner* will have a positive effect on student achievement when the standards are translated into the teaching and learning that happens every day in the library and classrooms of the school. The learning skills, dispositions, responsibilities, and self-assessment strategies presented in these standards must be explicitly taught by SLMSs and classroom teachers in the context of classroom curricula. Students and teachers will find that content learning is enhanced as students develop their repertoire of skills, strategies, and attitudes, as well as their commitment toward learning.

To facilitate the process of bringing the *Standards for the 21st-Century Learner* alive in school instructional programs, the following sections present action examples for library units and lessons on the new learning standards. The examples have been divided into sections by the benchmark years of grades 2, 5, 8, 10, and 12. All benchmark-year sections include the skills that might be taught at those grades to help students develop complex and sophisticated learning skills over the course of their years in school, with the goal of adequately preparing students for future learning

opportunities in higher education, the workplace, and personal life. In addition, each section includes action examples: sample lessons with descriptions of their instructional context. Following the action examples, a template is provided; SLMSs can use this template when creating their own units and lessons.

The action examples represent a variety of content areas, library contexts, and collaboration levels to outline possibilities for implementation of the *Standards for the 21st-Century Learner* in any school situation. Although no library professional would recommend limited collaboration or fixed scheduling, these are indeed realities confronted by SLMSs every day. The variety of instructional situations presented in the action examples is intended to support SLMSs in all types of school environments as they teach to the standards. No action example is intended to be prescriptive or complete, but each is offered as a framework upon which SLMSs can build instructional programs that support all students in their development as empowered 21st-century learners.

The following grid outlines the action examples included in the following sections.

GRADE	SKILL	DISPOSITION	RESPONSIBILITY	SELF-ASSESSMENT	CONTENT AREA	CONTENT TOPIC	LIBRARY CONTEXT	LEVEL OF COLLABORATION
K	1.1.2	3.3.5	2.3.1	2.4.3	Language Arts/ Health/ Social Studies	Community Helpers	Flexible; Lesson in a unit	Moderate
1	3.1.1 3.1.3 3.1.4	2.2.4	1.3.4	1.4.2	Science	Insect investigation	Flexible; Multiple lessons in a unit	Moderate
2	1.1.1 1.1.3 1.1.4 1.1.6	1.2.1 1.2.3 1.2.5 1.2.6	1.3.3 1.3.5	1.4.2 1.4.4 2.4.1 2.4.3	History	African American history	Flexible; Multiple lessons in a unit	Intensive
3	1.1.6	2.2.4	NA	1.4.4	Political Science/ Civics	Branches of U.S. government	Combination; Stand-alone lesson	Limited
4	2.1.6	2.2.4	1.3.5	3.4.2	Science/ Technology	Parts of a food web	Fixed; Stand-alone lesson	None
5	1.1.3	1.2.1	NA	2.4.2 3.4.2	Health	Nutritional value of snack foods	Fixed; Lesson in a unit	Intensive
6	3.1.5	2.2.4	2.3.1	4.4.5	Science	Energy sources and the environment	Flexible; Multiple lessons in a unit	Intensive
7	1.1.4 1.1.5	1.2.1 1.2.4	1.3.3	1.4.1 1.4.3	Social Studies/ Language Arts/ Technology	Community history	Flexible; Multiple lessons in a unit	Intensive
8	3.1.4 3.1.6	2.2.4 3.2.1	3.3.5 3.3.7	1.4.1 3.4.2	Science/Math/ Language Arts	Global warming	Combination; Multiple lessons in a unit	Moderate
9	4.1.7	4.2.1 4.2.2	4.3.1 4.3.4	1.4.2 1.4.4 4.4.1	English/ Technology	Favorite author	Individualized instruction	None
10	2.1.4	2.2.3	3.3.4	1.4.3	Math	Comparing data using InspireData software	Flexible; Stand-alone	Limited
11-12	4.1.3	3.2.3	3.3.7	2.4.2	English/ Language Arts	Relationship between a culture and its folklore	Flexible; Multiple lessons in a unit	Intensive

STRAND 1.1: SKILLS

STANDARD 1: Inquire, think critically and gain knowledge.

INDICATOR 1.1.1: Follow an inquiry-based process in seeking knowledge in curricular subjects, and make the real-world connection for using this process in own life.

– Form simple questions and begin to explore ways to answer them.

INDICATOR 1.1.2: Use prior and background knowledge as context for new learning.

– Connect ideas to personal experiences.
– Identify one or two keywords about a topic, problem, or question.
– Share what is known about a topic, problem, or question.

INDICATOR 1.1.3: Develop and refine a range of questions to frame the search for new understanding.

– Formulate questions related to listening activities.
– Ask "I wonder" questions about the topic, question, or problem.

INDICATOR 1.1.4: Find, evaluate, and select appropriate sources to answer questions.

– Understand the basic organizational structure of books.
– Distinguish between fiction and nonfiction books.
– Understand that the library has an organizational scheme.
– Select and use appropriate sources, including picture dictionaries, beginning encyclopedias, magazines, maps, and globes, to answer questions.

INDICATOR 1.1.5: Evaluate information found in selected sources on the basis of accuracy, validity, appropriateness for needs, importance, and social and cultural context.

– Recognize and use facts that answer specific questions.
– Interpret information represented in pictures, illustrations, and simple charts.

INDICATOR 1.1.6: Read, view, and listen for information presented in any format (for example, textual, visual, media, digital) in order to make inferences and gather meaning.

– Use simple note-taking strategies as demonstrated by SLMS.
– Write, draw, or verbalize the main idea and supporting details.

INDICATOR 1.1.7: Make sense of information gathered from diverse sources by identifying misconceptions, main and supporting ideas, conflicting information, and point of view or bias.

– Summarize or retell key points.

INDICATOR 1.1.8: Demonstrate mastery of technology tools for accessing information and pursuing inquiry.

– Recognize the purpose of the online catalog to locate materials.
– Use online encyclopedias and magazine databases with guidance.

INDICATOR 1.1.9: Collaborate with others to broaden and deepen understanding.

– Listen to others with respect.
– Share knowledge and ideas with others through discussion and listening.

STRAND 2.1: SKILLS

STANDARD 2: Draw conclusions, make informed decisions, apply knowledge to new situations, and create new knowledge.

INDICATOR 2.1.1:

Continue an inquiry-based research process by applying critical-thinking skills (analysis, synthesis, evaluation, organization) to information and knowledge in order to construct new understandings, draw conclusions, and create new knowledge.

- Answer the question, "What is this mostly about?"
- Find facts to answer questions in more than one source.
- Note similarities and differences in information from different sources.
- Identify supporting details.

INDICATOR 2.1.2:

Organize knowledge so that it is useful.

- Demonstrate simple organizational skills, such as sorting and categorizing.
- Organize information into different forms (charts, drawings).

INDICATOR 2.1.3:

Use strategies to draw conclusions from information and apply knowledge to curricular areas, real-world situations, and further investigations.

- Complete a graphic organizer using concepts that were learned during the inquiry experience.
- Compare new ideas with what was known at the beginning of the inquiry.
- With guidance make inferences regarding the topic at the conclusion of a theme or research project.
- With guidance draw a conclusion about the main idea.

INDICATOR 2.1.4:

Use technology and other information tools to analyze and organize information.

- Use word processing and drawing tools to create a final product.

INDICATOR 2.1.5:

Collaborate with others to exchange ideas, develop new understandings, make decisions, and solve problems.

- Share information and ideas with others by discussion and listening.
- Work in groups to create, share, and evaluate simple information products (poster, diorama).

INDICATOR 2.1.6:

Use the writing process, media and visual literacy, and technology skills to create products that express new understandings.

- Create a product with a beginning, middle, and end.
- Use basic grammar conventions.
- Incorporate writing and oral skills to develop a product or performance.
- Use pictures to communicate new information and ideas.
- Revise work with peer or teacher guidance.

STRAND 3.1: SKILLS

STANDARD 3: Share knowledge and participate ethically and productively as members of our democratic society.

INDICATOR 3.1.1:

Conclude an inquiry-based research process by sharing new understandings and reflecting on the learning.

- Present facts and simple answers to questions.
- Use simple rubrics to assess work.
- Reflect at the end of an inquiry experience about new ideas to wonder about and investigate.

(continues on page 66)

(continued from page 65)

INDICATOR 3.1.2: Participate and collaborate as members of a social and intellectual network of learners.

– Participate in discussions and listen well.

– Show respect for the ideas of others.

– Give positive feedback.

– Respect rules and procedures as responsible library users.

– Share favorite literature, both fiction and nonfiction.

– Begin to create collaborative projects.

– Share information and creative products with others, using diverse formats, both print and nonprint.

INDICATOR 3.1.3: Use writing and speaking skills to communicate new understandings effectively.

– Choose and maintain a focus in a piece of writing.

– Add details from personal experience and research to support ideas.

– Use a variety of ways (through art, music, movement, and oral and written language) to present information and main ideas; use oral and written language in a variety of formats (for example, narrative text, poetry, podcasts).

INDICATOR 3.1.4: Use technology and other information tools to organize and display knowledge and understanding in ways that others can view, use, and assess.

– Use word processing and drawing tools to organize and communicate ideas.

INDICATOR 3.1.5: Connect learning to community issues.

– Express personal connections to the topic or question.

– Identify how the topic or question relates to a real-world need.

INDICATOR 3.1.6: Use information and technology ethically and responsibly.

– Rephrase rather than copy whole sentences.

– Credit sources by citing author and title.

– Distinguish between acceptable and unacceptable computer use.

– Follow school guidelines related to the acceptable use of technology.

– Use technology in appropriate ways outside the school.

STRAND 4.1: SKILLS

STANDARD 4: Pursue personal and aesthetic growth.

INDICATOR 4.1.1: Read, view, and listen for pleasure and personal growth.

– Distinguish between what is real and what is not real.

– Request and choose materials related to personal interests.

– Read, view, and listen to a variety of fiction and nonfiction for enjoyment and information.

– Begin to recognize that different genres require different reading, listening, or viewing strategies.

INDICATOR 4.1.2: Read widely and fluently to make connections with self, the world, and previous reading.

– Read widely from multicultural texts in various genres to find out about self and the surrounding world.

– Predict what will happen next in a story.

- Draw conclusions about main idea of a story.

- Identify author's purpose and connect illustrations to a story.

- Compare and contrast characters in two different stories or plots in two stories by the same author.

- Retell a story using their own words and pictures.

INDICATOR 4.1.3:	Respond to literature and creative expressions of ideas in various formats and genres.

- Express feelings about characters and events in a story.

- Make connections between literature and their own experiences.

- Write about or orally share reactions to imaginative stories and performances.

- Retell stories using the correct sequence of events.

- Identify plot, characters, times, and places in a story.

- Discuss favorite books and authors.

INDICATOR 4.1.4:	Seek information for personal learning in a variety of formats and genres.

- Routinely select picture, fiction, and information books; try some books in other genres (poetry, fairy tales).

- Select information in various formats and genres based on suggestions from teacher or SLMS and on personal interest.

- Select some books at the appropriate reading level, other books to be read aloud, and other more challenging books of particular interest for browsing and enjoyment.

- Explain personal criteria for selecting a particular resource.

INDICATOR 4.1.5:	Connect ideas to own interests and previous knowledge and experience.

- Prior to reading a book, gain background knowledge about the author or subject by discussing it with friend, teacher, or parent.

- Demonstrate comprehension of stories read independently or shared aloud.

- Develop criteria for deciding if a book matches interests and reading levels.

- Find and read (or be read) books that match interests and comprehension levels.

INDICATOR 4.1.6:	Organize personal knowledge in a way that can be called upon easily.

- Take notes using graphic organizer provided by teacher or SLMS.

- Draw pictures of main ideas.

INDICATOR 4.1.7:	Use social networks and information tools to gather and share information.

- Locate information for personal interests and school assignments in print, nonprint, and electronic sources with guidance from the SLMS.

- Experiment with online catalog and Web resources to locate information.

INDICATOR 4.1.8:	Use creative and artistic formats to express personal learning.

- Express feelings about a story through pictures and words.

- Use technology tools to create and present ideas.

- Express their own ideas through simple products in different formats.

ACTION EXAMPLE: KINDERGARTEN

GRADE: K

LIBRARY CONTEXT:

- ☐ Fixed
- ■ Flexible
- ☐ Combination
- ☐ Individualized instruction
- ☐ Stand-alone lesson
- ■ Lesson in a unit
- ☐ Multiple lessons in a unit

COLLABORATION CONTINUUM:

- ☐ None
- ☐ Limited
- ■ Moderate
- ☐ Intensive

CONTENT TOPIC:

Community Helpers

ESTIMATED LESSON TIME:

30 Minutes

Standards for the 21st-Century Learner Goals

STANDARD 1: Inquire, think critically and gain knowledge.

SKILLS INDICATOR:

1.1.2 Use prior and background knowledge as context for new learning.

BENCHMARKS:

- Connect ideas to personal experiences.
- Share what is known about a topic, problem or question.

DISPOSITIONS INDICATOR:

3.3.5 Contribute to the exchange of ideas within and beyond the learning community.

RESPONSIBILITIES INDICATOR:

2.3.1 Connect understanding to the real world.

SELF-ASSESSMENT STRATEGIES INDICATOR:

2.4.3 Recognize new knowledge and understanding.

SCENARIO:

When meeting with the kindergarten teachers during their monthly planning meeting, the SLMS participates in the planning of an upcoming unit on community helpers and what they do for our community. The curriculum objectives state that students should not only be able to name various community helpers, such as the doctor, nurse, policeman, firefighter, teacher, and principal, but also identify what helpers contribute through their actions to make them a vital part of our community. The SLMS states that several available literature choices will support these objectives and volunteers to work with the teachers to create a lesson. The SLMS goes on to brainstorm with the teachers on this lesson idea. They agree that the SLMS will identify appropriate resources for the team, select literature for the lesson, and design a graphic organizer that will be used on the interactive whiteboard during the lesson. The teachers plan to introduce the unit and then visit the media center for a lesson during the second week of the unit. Following the lesson, the teachers will continue to build on what students have learned and also identify areas where students might need further assistance. Since flexible scheduling is in place, each teacher will sign up for a time that works for her class.

CONNECTION TO LOCAL OR STATE STANDARDS:

Content Standards for Grade K Social Studies: The student can identify various workers and their jobs in the community.

Content Standards for Grade K Health: The student can name people in the school and community who provide health support for others.

Content Standards for Grade K Language Arts: The student can use knowledge of the conventions of language and texts to construct meaning for a range of literary and informational texts for a variety of purposes.

OVERVIEW:

In a theme unit on community helpers, kindergarten students will name a range of community helpers and be able to describe how they perform their major roles. The essential questions for this unit include: Who are community helpers? How do they help us?

FINAL PRODUCT:

Students complete an SLMS-created graphic organizer that connects community helpers with the tools they need to do their jobs. Each student will choose one helper to explain how he or she uses tools in the role played in the community.

LIBRARY LESSON:

Students will learn that they need to recall prior knowledge from their own experiences and classroom learning.

ASSESSMENT

Product: SLMS and teacher assess the completed graphic organizers looking for correct match of helpers with tools; the SLMS and teacher also use a checklist to assess each student's understanding of how the chosen community helper uses tools to make a contribution to the community.

Process: SLMS and teacher observe students as they work on their graphic organizers and listen as they describe the connection between the tools their chosen community helpers use and the helpers' roles in the community.

Student self-questioning:

– Did I understand my task?
– Did I listen carefully enough to find the information I need?
– Did I use information I already knew?
– Did I participate and contribute to the group learning activity?

INSTRUCTIONAL PLAN

Resources students will use:

☐ Online subscription database(s)

☐ Websites

■ Books

☐ Reference

☐ Nonprint

☐ Periodicals/newspapers

☐ Other (list):

INSTRUCTION/ACTIVITIES

Direct instruction: As class comes in, engage students by showing on the interactive whiteboard a rotating display of the covers of books chosen for the lesson and of photographs of community helpers. Begin with a discussion about what students know about community helpers from personal experience or from classroom instruction. SLMS and teacher review with students what they have been learning in their classroom to make connections and identify purpose for the lesson. The SLMS then reads the literature selection, questioning and emphasizing keys points throughout the story.

Modeling and guided practice: SLMS explains the graphic organizer and demonstrates how to use it and the interactive whiteboard by modeling an example with the teacher.

Independent practice: To demonstrate what they have learned by accurately completing the graphic organizer, students volunteer to come up to the whiteboard and connect the community helper picture with the tools needed to do his or her job.

Sharing and reflecting: Students each chose one helper and explain to the group how the helper uses those tools to play his or her part in a community.

GRADE: 1

LIBRARY CONTEXT:

☐ Fixed

■ Flexible

☐ Combination

☐ Individualized instruction

☐ Stand-alone lesson

☐ Lesson in a unit

■ Multiple lessons in a unit

COLLABORATION CONTINUUM:

☐ None

☐ Limited

■ Moderate

☐ Intensive

CONTENT TOPIC:

Insect Investigation

ESTIMATED LESSON TIME:

5 Sessions 30–60 minutes

Standards for the 21st-Century Learner Goals

STANDARD 3: Share knowledge and participate ethically and productively as members of our democratic society.

SKILLS INDICATORS:

3.1.1 Conclude an inquiry-based research process by sharing new understandings and reflecting on the learning.

3.1.3 Use writing and speaking skills to communicate new understandings effectively.

3.1.4 Use technology and other information tools to organize and display knowledge and understanding in ways that others can view, use, and assess.

BENCHMARKS:

– Use simple rubrics to assess work.

– Use a variety of ways (through art, music, movement, and oral and written language) to present information and main ideas; use oral and written language in a variety of formats (for example, narrative text, poetry, podcasts).

– Use word processing and drawing tools to organize and communicate ideas.

DISPOSITIONS INDICATOR:

2.2.4 Demonstrate personal productivity by completing products to express learning.

RESPONSIBILITIES INDICATOR:

1.3.4 Contribute to the exchange of ideas within the learning community.

SELF-ASSESSMENT STRATEGIES INDICATOR:

1.4.2 Use interaction with and feedback from teachers and peers to guide own inquiry process.

SCENARIO:

First-graders discover a strange-looking insect on the school playground during recess. Their teacher captures the bug in a jar and asks for three student volunteers to be the "bug detectives" for the class. She enlists the help of the SLMS to assist the trio. The students and the SLMS browse through the library's resources with no luck. Ultimately, the SLMS helps the students e-mail an entomologist at the local university, who identifies the insect as an assassin bug. This really excites the students and motivates them to search for more information. The SLMS not only helps the students gather details on the bug, but she gets the technology resource teacher to help the students prepare a two-minute video on the bug for airing on the school's closed circuit television system. The SLMS takes the lead in working with the three students as they draft their script, rehearse it, and critique their work before taping it. The teacher releases these students to work in the library while other students in the class are working on science-related activities

CONNECTION TO LOCAL OR STATE STANDARDS:

Content Standards for Grade 1 Science: The student can ask questions about objects, organisms, events, places, or relationships in the environment.

Content Standards for Grade 1 Language Arts: The student can construct meaning by asking and answering who, what, when, why, where, and how questions about what is read.

Content Standards for Grade 1 Language Arts: The student can present ideas in a logical order or sequence that is easy to follow.

Content Standards for Grade 1 Technology: The student can demonstrate creative thinking and construct knowledge using technology.

OVERVIEW:

First-grade students undertake a mini-investigation in which they identify a strange-looking insect, collect information on the insect, and communicate their findings to the rest of their class and the entire school. The young investigators fashion their presentation around the essential questions: What should people know about this insect? Why would it be important for people to know these facts about it?

FINAL PRODUCT:

Students develop a two-minute video on their findings that is aired on closed circuit television.

LIBRARY LESSONS:

Students work with the SLMS in a series of five sessions focusing on the creation of the video presentation. In these sessions the students collaboratively select the major facts they wish to share about the insect, divide the scripting work, draft the segments, rehearse the parts, and critique each other's performance.

ASSESSMENT

Product: Classmates critique the final video performance using a simple rubric devised by the SLMS. The rubric includes criteria on content accuracy, organization, delivery, and visual support used.

Process: The SLMS and the three students producing the video also use the same rubric to critique performances during rehearsals.

Student self-questioning:
– Are all my facts correct?
– Will others understand my message?
– Am I making the presentation interesting?

INSTRUCTIONAL PLAN

Resources students will use:

☐ Online subscription database(s)

■ Websites

■ Books

☐ Reference

☐ Nonprint

☐ Periodicals/newspapers

☐ Other (list):

INSTRUCTION/ACTIVITIES

Note: This particular session focuses on having the students analyze their writing and speaking skills as they rehearse for the video performance.

Direct Instruction: Tap prior knowledge by asking students what would make a good video performance. Create a list. Share the rubric created by the SLMS and compare the criteria on the rubric with the list that the students have contributed. Go over the criteria together.

Modeling and guided practice: Have the students use the rubric to critique the SLMS as she models a mock performance that requires more work. Share the critiques.

Independent practice: Have each student, in turn, rehearse his or her performance. Along with the SLMS the students critique each other's performance using the rubric.

Sharing and reflecting: As a group, the students and SLMS exchange critiques. Have students identify areas where they did well and areas that they need to work on. Encourage them to practice in front of their families at home and invite critiquing of performances.

ACTION EXAMPLE: GRADE 2

GRADE: 2

LIBRARY CONTEXT:

☐ Fixed

■ Flexible

☐ Combination

☐ Individualized instruction

☐ Stand-alone lesson

☐ Lesson in a unit

■ Multiple lessons in a unit

COLLABORATION CONTINUUM:

☐ None

☐ Limited

☐ Moderate

■ Intensive

CONTENT TOPIC:

African American History

ESTIMATED LESSON TIME:

4 Sessions time varies per session

Standards for the 21st-Century Learner Goals

STANDARD 1: Inquire, think critically, and gain knowledge.

SKILLS INDICATORS:

1.1.1 Follow an inquiry-based process in seeking knowledge in curricular subjects, and make the real-world connection for using this process in own life.

1.1.3 Develop and refine a range of questions to frame the search for new understanding.

1.1.4 Find, evaluate, and select appropriate sources to answer questions.

1.1.6 Read, view and listen for information presented in any format (e.g., textual, visual, media, digital) in order to make inferences and gather meaning.

BENCHMARKS:

– Form simple questions and begin to explore ways to answer them.

– Ask "I wonder" questions about the topic, question, or problem.

– Select and use appropriate sources, including picture dictionaries, beginning encyclopedias, magazines, maps, and globes, to answer questions.

– Write, draw, or verbalize the main idea and supporting details.

DISPOSITIONS INDICATORS:

1.2.1 Display initiative and engagement by posing questions and investigating the answers beyond the collection of superficial facts.

1.2.3 Demonstrate creativity by using multiple resources and formats.

1.2.5 Demonstrate adaptability by changing the inquiry focus, questions, resources, or strategies when necessary to achieve success.

1.2.6 Display emotional resilience by persisting in information searching despite challenges.

RESPONSIBILITIES INDICATORS:

1.3.3 Follow ethical and legal guidelines in gathering and using information.

1.3.5 Use information technology responsibly.

SELF-ASSESSMENT STRATEGIES INDICATORS:

1.4.2 Use interaction with and feedback from teachers and peers to guide own inquiry process.

1.4.4 Seek appropriate help when it is needed.

2.4.1 Determine how to act on information (accept, reject, modify).

2.4.3 Recognize new knowledge and understanding.

The SLMS meets with teachers at each grade level during their planning meetings at least once a month. Second-grade teachers ask the SLMS to help them plan the final social studies unit of the year, which covers famous African American historical figures. The SLMS suggests that this would be a great opportunity to reinforce some information literacy skills previously taught in the year and to address additional skills with a research process project. Since these students have already completed some minor projects this year, they have previous experience in working with graphic organizers, reading biographies, using tables of contents and indexes, locating information in encyclopedias, and taking notes.

The SLMS and the teachers work together to plan the unit and to decide the role each will play in the teaching and assessment. The teachers will introduce the unit with a book about Rosa Parks, and with a basic streaming video about famous African Americans and the struggle for civil rights. The SLMS and teachers create a list of historical names based on curricular standards. The teacher will have students choose a historical figure and will introduce the project before coming to the media center. The teachers and the SLMS work together to create a graphic organizer that the students will use to organize the information they find. Research questions will be developed through a guided brainstorming activity. The SLMS will pull all related materials for this project and house them on a reserve shelf for the students. For each famous person the SLMS will also create a hotlist of websites that students can access at school or at home. The SLMS and teachers work together to create assessment rubrics. Since flexible scheduling is in place, teachers work with the SLMS to schedule the various lessons and research time.

CONNECTION TO LOCAL OR STATE STANDARDS:

Content Standards for Grade 2 Social Studies: The students will read about and describe the lives of historical figures in history.

Content Standards for Grade 2 Social Studies: The student will give examples of how historical figures under study demonstrate positive citizenship traits (honesty, dependability, persistence, honor, civility).

Content Standards for Grade 2 Language Arts: The student can use knowledge of the conventions of language and texts to construct meaning for a range of literary and informational texts for a variety of purposes.

Content Standards for Grade 2 Language Arts: The students will use the writing process and conventions of language and research to construct meaning and communicate effectively for a variety of purposes and audiences using a range of forms.

OVERVIEW:

In a second-grade unit on famous African Americans in history, students will apply the research process in a major project that involves several lessons.

FINAL PRODUCT:

The project culminates in a final typed essay, a portrait picture of the famous African American, and a presentation to the class of this work.

LIBRARY LESSONS:

Students work with the SLMS in a series of four sessions during which students will learn how to (1) develop questions that relate to and are of importance to their topic, (2) select a variety of resources to retrieve relevant information, (3) use a graphic organizer to organize the information collected, and (4) assess information to decide if it meets their needs.

ASSESSMENT

Product: SLMS, teacher, and students assess final papers and presentations using rubrics that focus on main ideas and supporting details, organization, and language.

Process: SLMS and teacher review graphic organizers and conference notes completed by students to determine whether students (1) chose appropriate sources and information to fit their needs, (2) adapted as necessary, (3) named sources they used correctly, and (4) put information in their own words.

Student self-questioning:

- Did I understand my task?
- Was I able to come up with questions that were important to and related to my topic?
- Was I able to successfully use different resources to locate the information I needed?
- Was I able to determine if information I found answered my questions?
- Was I able to adapt my searching when needed?
- Did I ask for help when I needed it?

INSTRUCTIONAL PLAN

Resources students will use:

- ■ Online subscription database(s)
- ■ Websites
- ■ Books
- ■ Reference
- ■ Nonprint
- ☐ Periodicals/newspapers
- ☐ Other (list):

INSTRUCTION/ACTIVITIES

Lesson 1

Direct Instruction: The SLMS and teacher review with the class what was learned earlier in the year about developing questions to guide research.

Modeling and guided practice: The SLMS and teacher use an interactive whiteboard to brainstorm questions with the class about what is important to know about their historical figures. Ideas are listed on the whiteboard.

Independent practice: On their graphic organizers students write the three questions they think are most important.

Sharing and reflecting: The class discusses the questions they have chosen and come to consensus on the three main questions they will answer about their historical figures.

Lessons 2 and 3

Direct Instruction: The SLMS and teacher explain a checklist they will use to conference with each student to see how they are progressing.

Modeling and guided practice: The SLMS follows this review with some examples to refresh students' memory, emphasizing how to decide if something they read is important and related to their topic.

Independent practice: Students use the remaining time in this visit to browse through resources for needed information. The next time they come to the library, they use the various resources in the media center, including a website list, to locate information.

Sharing and reflecting: On a card each student writes down the best source found and why it is the best one; before returning to class, the students give the cards to the SLMS.

Lesson 4

Direct Instruction: The SLMS and teacher explain a checklist they will use while conferencing with each student to see how he or she is progressing.

Modeling and guided practice: Using the checklist students have completed prior to their conferences, the SLMS and teacher help the students determine their problem areas and provide guidance as needed.

Independent practice: While the SLMS or teacher conference with individual students, the rest of the class continues to use various resources to locate information. Should students require more time to complete their information gathering, their teacher will allow them to visit the media center to work independently or with assistance from the SLMS.

Sharing and reflecting: Students complete their checklists to monitor their own progress and uncover problem areas with which they need assistance.

B SKILL BENCHMARKS TO ACHIEVE BY GRADE 5

STRAND 1.1: SKILLS

STANDARD 1: Inquire, think critically and gain knowledge.

INDICATOR 1.1.1:

Follow an inquiry-based process in seeking knowledge in curricular subjects, and make the real-world connection for using this process in own life.

- Generate questions and practice different ways to locate and evaluate sources that provide needed information.

INDICATOR 1.1.2:

Use prior and background knowledge as context for new learning.

- Connect ideas or topics to their own interests.
- Articulate what is known about a topic, problem or question.
- With guidance generate a list of keywords for an inquiry-based project.
- Identify and use appropriate sources to acquire background information.
- Predict answers to inquiry questions based on background knowledge and beginning observations or experiences.

INDICATOR 1.1.3:

Develop and refine a range of questions to frame the search for new understanding.

- With guidance formulate questions about the topic.
- Assess questions to determine which can be answered by simple facts, which cannot be answered, and which would lead to an interesting inquiry.
- Revise the question or problem as needed to arrive at a manageable topic.

INDICATOR 1.1.4:

Find, evaluate, and select appropriate sources to answer questions.

- Understand the library's organizational scheme and what main topics are included in each section.
- Select and use appropriate sources, including specialized reference sources and databases, to answer questions.
- Use multiple resources, including print, electronic, and human, to locate information.
- Use the organizational structure of a book (for example, table of contents, index, chapter headings) to locate information to answer questions.
- Use text features and illustrations to decide which resources are best to use and why.

INDICATOR 1.1.5:

Evaluate information found in selected sources on the basis of accuracy, validity, appropriateness for needs, importance, and social and cultural context.

- Skim/scan to locate information that is appropriate to age and ability level.
- Identify facts and details that support main ideas.
- Evaluate facts for accuracy.
- Distinguish between fact and opinion.
- Interpret information taken from maps, graphs, charts, and other visuals.
- Select information to answer questions or solve a problem.

INDICATOR 1.1.6:

Read, view, and listen for information presented in any format (for example, textual, visual, media, digital) in order to make inferences and gather meaning.

- Use various note-taking strategies (for example, outlining, questioning the text, highlighting, graphic organizers).

(continues on page 76)

(continued from page 75)

– Paraphrase or summarize information in various formats.

– Draw conclusions based on facts and premises.

INDICATOR 1.1.7: | **Make sense of information gathered from diverse sources by identifying misconceptions, main and supporting ideas, conflicting information, and point of view or bias.**

– Recognize when facts from two different sources conflict and seek additional sources to verify accuracy.

– Recognize their own misconceptions when new information conflicts with previously held opinions.

INDICATOR 1.1.8: | **Demonstrate mastery of technology tools for accessing information and pursuing inquiry.**

– Search an online catalog to locate materials.

– Use selected websites and periodical databases to find appropriate information.

– Use selected search engines to find appropriate information.

– Use software or online tools to record and organize information.

INDICATOR 1.1.9: | **Collaborate with others to broaden and deepen understanding.**

– Work in teams to produce original works or solve problems.

– Respect others' opinions through active listening and questioning.

STANDARD 2: Draw conclusions, make informed decisions, apply knowledge to new situations, and create new knowledge.

STRAND 2.1: SKILLS

INDICATOR 2.1.1: | **Continue an inquiry-based research process by applying critical-thinking skills (analysis, synthesis, evaluation, organization) to information and knowledge in order to construct new understandings, draw conclusions, and create new knowledge.**

– Use different clues (placement in text, signal words, focal point of illustration) to determine important ideas in illustrations and text.

– Identify facts and details that support main ideas.

– Restate and respond with detailed answers to factual questions.

– Find similar big ideas in more than one source.

– With guidance make inferences.

INDICATOR 2.1.2: | **Organize knowledge so that it is useful.**

– Organize notes and ideas to form responses to questions.

– Organize the information in a way that is appropriate for the assignment or question.

– Use common organizational patterns (chronological order, main idea with supporting ideas) to make sense of information.

INDICATOR 2.1.3: | **Use strategies to draw conclusions from information and apply knowledge to curricular areas, real-world situations, and further investigations.**

– Review ideas held at beginning of inquiry and reflections captured during note taking.

– Match information found with questions and predictions.

– Make inferences about the topic at the conclusion of a research project.

– Draw a conclusion about the main idea.

– Identify connections to the curriculum and real world.

INDICATOR 2.1.4: Use technology and other information tools to analyze and organize information.

– Use word processing, drawing, presentation, graphing, and other productivity tools to illustrate concepts and convey ideas.

INDICATOR 2.1.5: Collaborate with others to exchange ideas, develop new understandings, make decisions, and solve problems.

– Express their own ideas appropriately and effectively while working in groups to identify and resolve information problems.

– Work in groups to create and evaluate pictures, images, and charts for word processed reports and electronic presentations.

INDICATOR 2.1.6: Use the writing process, media and visual literacy, and technology skills to create products that express new understandings.

– Follow steps of the writing/creation process: prewriting, drafting, revising, editing, and publishing.

– Identify the audience and purpose before selecting a format for the product.

– Experiment with text and visual media to create products.

– Edit drafts based on feedback.

– Check for correctness, completeness, and citation of sources.

STRAND 3.1: SKILLS

STANDARD 3: Share knowledge and participate ethically and productively as members of our democratic society.

INDICATOR 3.1.1: Conclude an inquiry-based research process by sharing new understandings and reflecting on the learning.

– Present information clearly so that main points are evident.

– Use information appropriate to task and audience.

– Identify and evaluate the important features for a good product.

– Identify their own strengths and set goals for improvement.

– Reflect at the end of an inquiry experience about what ideas would still be interesting to pursue.

INDICATOR 3.1.2: Participate and collaborate as members of a social and intellectual network of learners.

– Show respect for and respond to ideas of others.

– Accurately describe or restate ideas of others.

– Acknowledge personal and group achievements.

– Rely on feedback to improve product and process.

– Respect the guidelines for responsible and ethical use of information resources.

– Share favorite literature.

– Participate in discussions on fiction and nonfiction related to curriculum.

– Develop a product with peers and share with others.

– Develop projects with peers that can be shared electronically and can challenge other students to answer questions or give opinions adding to the content (for example, shared book reviews, shared slide presentations).

(continues on page 78)

(continued from page 77)

INDICATOR 3.1.3: | **Use writing and speaking skills to communicate new understandings effectively.**

– Use significant details and relevant information to develop meaning.

– Present information coherently in oral, written, and visual sequence.

– Use clear and appropriate vocabulary to convey the intended message.

– Speak clearly to convey meaning.

INDICATOR 3.1.4: | **Use technology and other information tools to organize and display knowledge and understanding in ways that others can view, use, and assess.**

– Use various technology tools to retrieve and organize information.

– Use a variety of media and formats to create and edit products that communicate syntheses of information and ideas.

INDICATOR 3.1.5: | **Connect learning to community issues.**

– Gather ideas and information from different points of view.

– Base opinions on information from multiple sources of authority.

– Examine the concept of freedom of speech and explain why it is important.

– Connect ideas and information to situations and people in the larger community.

INDICATOR 3.1.6: | **Use information and technology ethically and responsibly.**

– Demonstrate understanding of plagiarism by paraphrasing information or noting direct quotes.

– Understand that authors and illustrators own their writings and art and it is against the law to copy their work.

– Credit all sources properly with title, author, and page number.

– Observe Web safety procedures including safeguarding personal information.

– Practice responsible use of technology and describe personal consequences of inappropriate use.

– Respect privacy of others (e-mail, files, passwords, book checkout, etc.).

STRAND 4.1: SKILLS | **STANDARD 4: Pursue personal and aesthetic growth.**

INDICATOR 4.1.1: | **Read, view, and listen for pleasure and personal growth.**

– Set reading goals.

– Read, listen to, and view a range of resources for a variety of purposes: to live the experiences of a character, to answer questions, to find out about something new, to explore personal interests.

– Visit the public library to attend programs, seek help as needed, and check out materials to read.

INDICATOR 4.1.2: | **Read widely and fluently to make connections with self, the world, and previous reading.**

– Use evidence from the text to discuss the author's purpose.

– Read widely to explore new ideas.

– Predict and infer about events and characters.

– Identify problems and solutions in a story.

- Draw conclusions about the theme of a story.
- Describe how an illustrator's style and use of elements and media represent and extend the meaning of the story or the narrative text.
- Connect story to previous reading.
- Recognize features of various genres and use different reading strategies for understanding.
- Demonstrate knowledge of favorite authors and genres.

INDICATOR 4.1.3: | **Respond to literature and creative expressions of ideas in various formats and genres.**

- Connect their own feelings to emotions, characters, and events portrayed in a literary work.
- Use personal experiences to stimulate responses to literature and art.
- Restate and interpret ideas presented through creative formats.
- Identify story elements in various fiction genres.
- Use evidence from stories to discuss characters, setting, plot, time, and place.
- Discuss theme of stories, using evidence to support opinions.
- Participate in book talks and book discussion groups.

INDICATOR 4.1.4: | **Seek information for personal learning in a variety of formats and genres.**

- Select books from favorite authors and genres; try new genres when suggested.
- Select information in various formats based on a theme, topic, and connection to classroom learning or personal interest.
- Routinely select both "just right" books and challenging books.
- Read multiple works of a single author.
- Explain why some authors and genres have become favorites.
- Independently select appropriate print, nonprint, and electronic materials on an individual level.

INDICATOR 4.1.5: | **Connect ideas to own interests and previous knowledge and experience.**

- Use prior knowledge to understand and compare literature.
- Understand literal meaning and identify the main points reflected in a work.
- Compare the ideas in various types of resources to experiences in real life.

INDICATOR 4.1.6: | **Organize personal knowledge in a way that can be called upon easily.**

- Use simple graphic organizers and technology tools to capture the main ideas and their relationships to each other.
- Use two-column approach to note taking to capture personal connections to information.

INDICATOR 4.1.7: | **Use social networks and information tools to gather and share information.**

- Use basic strategies (author, title, subject) to locate information using the library's online catalog.
- Use social networking tools to create and share information.

INDICATOR 4.1.8: | **Use creative and artistic formats to express personal learning.**

- Present creative products in a variety of formats.
- Use technology applications to create documents and visualizations of new learning.
- Use multimedia authoring tools for independent and collaborative publishing activities.

ACTION EXAMPLE: GRADE 3

GRADE: 3

LIBRARY CONTEXT:

☐ Fixed

☐ Flexible

■ Combination

☐ Individualized instruction

■ Stand-alone lesson

☐ Lesson in a unit

☐ Multiple lessons in a unit

COLLABORATION CONTINUUM:

☐ None

■ Limited

☐ Moderate

☐ Intensive

CONTENT TOPIC:

Branches of the United States Government

ESTIMATED LESSON TIME:

30 Minutes

Standards for the 21st-Century Learner Goals

STANDARD 1: Inquire, think critically and gain knowledge.

SKILLS INDICATOR:

1.1.6 Read, view, and listen for information presented in any format (for example, textual, visual, media, digital) in order to make inferences and gather meaning.

BENCHMARKS:

– Use various note-taking strategies (for example, outlining, questioning the text, highlighting, graphic organizers).

– Paraphrase or summarize information in various formats.

DISPOSITIONS INDICATORS:

2.2.4 Demonstrate personal productivity by completing products to express learning.

RESPONSIBILITIES INDICATORS:

NA

SELF-ASSESSMENT STRATEGIES INDICATOR:

1.4.4 Seek appropriate help when it is needed.

SCENARIO:

Third-grade teachers have informed the SLMS that they are ready to begin their annual unit on the U.S. government. The teachers want their students to be able to name the three branches of government, the officials, and the responsibilities of each branch. They have requested that the SLMS, as he has done in previous years, introduce the unit to the students with the Schoolhouse Rock song and video "Three-Ring Government." During their weekly forty-minute library class, the SLMS guides the students in listening and watching for these facts. Each student, with assistance from the SLMS, fills in a graphic organizer matching the name of each branch with its officials and major responsibilities. The SLMS also prepares a display of fiction and nonfiction books related to the topic; students may browse and borrow these books during their ten-minute book-selection time at the end of the class. The third-grade teachers continue with further instruction in their classrooms. In subsequent specially arranged library visits the SLMS assists students in selecting resources for assignments on this topic.

CONNECTION TO LOCAL OR STATE STANDARDS:

Content Standards for Grade 3 Social Studies: The students can describe the purpose and structures of the three branches of the federal government.

Content Standards for Grade 3 Language Arts: The student can explain the results of an investigation to an audience using simple data organizers (for example, charts, graphs, pictures).

OVERVIEW:

In social studies class, third-grade students identify the structure of the federal government and describe the roles and responsibilities of U.S. government officials. The essential question framing the unit is: How is our government organized?

FINAL PRODUCT:

Each student completes a graphic organizer matching the names of the three branches of the federal government with the officials and major responsibilities of each branch.

LIBRARY LESSONS:

Students will learn to listen and watch for information, then record and categorize it using a graphic organizer.

ASSESSMENT

Product: Students complete an SLMS-created graphic organizer that resembles the three rings of a circus. They must (1) correctly identify the three government branches, (2) correctly list the officials for each branch, and (3) include one major responsibility of each branch.

Process: SLMS observes students as they work on their graphic organizers and work together to complete an accurate model.

Student self-questioning:

- Did I understand my task?
- Did I listen carefully enough to find the information I need?
- Did I complete the organizer with all of the information required?
- Did I place information correctly in the graphic organizer?
- Was all the information I included in the graphic organizer accurate?

INSTRUCTIONAL PLAN

Resources students will use:

☐ Online subscription database(s)

☐ Websites

☐ Books

☐ Reference

■ Nonprint: Schoolhouse Rock video, recording

☐ Periodicals/newspapers

■ Other (list): Song lyrics

INSTRUCTION/ACTIVITIES

Direct Instruction: The SLMS introduces the lesson by showing the students the Schoolhouse Rock video, "Three-Ring Government." Following the viewing of the video, the SLMS displays on an interactive whiteboard a list of words from the song that pertain to the branches of the government and discusses their definitions with the class.

Modeling and guided practice: The SLMS distributes the lyrics of the song to the class. While they listen to the song again, students raise their hands each time they hear a word about a branch of the government. The SLMS highlights these words on the whiteboard while the students circle them on their lyric sheets.

Independent practice: Following a second viewing of the video, students label the three rings on their graphic organizers with the names of each branch, and fill in the officials and major responsibility of the branches. The SLMS assists students who have questions.

Sharing and reflecting: When the students have completed their own graphic organizers, they take turns filling in the information on an organizer projected on the whiteboard. Together they determine the correct placement of all the labels. Then they check the accuracy of their own results by comparing them with the completed organizer.

ACTION EXAMPLE: GRADE 4

GRADE: 4

LIBRARY CONTEXT:

- ■ Fixed
- ☐ Flexible
- ☐ Combination
- ☐ Individualized instruction
- ■ Stand-alone lesson
- ☐ Lesson in a unit
- ☐ Multiple lessons in a unit

COLLABORATION CONTINUUM:

- ■ None
- ☐ Limited
- ☐ Moderate
- ☐ Intensive

CONTENT TOPIC:

Parts of the Food Web and Major Functions and Relationships Among the Parts

ESTIMATED LESSON TIME:

Two 45-minute lessons

Standards for the 21st-Century Learner Goals

STANDARD 2: Draw conclusions, make informed decisions, apply knowledge to new situations, and create new knowledge.

SKILLS INDICATOR:

2.1.6 Use the writing process, media and visual literacy, and technology skills to create products that express new understandings.

BENCHMARK:

– Follow steps of the writing/creation process: prewriting, drafting, revising, editing, and publishing.

DISPOSITIONS INDICATOR:

2.2.4 Demonstrate personal productivity by completing products to express learning.

RESPONSIBILITIES INDICATOR:

1.3.5 Use information technology responsibly.

SELF-ASSESSMENT STRATEGIES INDICATOR:

3.4.2 Assess the quality and effectiveness of the learning product.

SCENARIO:

An SLMS uses long range planning forms to prepare for an activity with a fourth-grade class. The students are nearing the end of a science unit on ecology. The SLMS divides the students into teams of three and escorts them to the green space surrounding the school. Each team is given a digital camera and the direction to photograph producers, consumers, and decomposers for the purpose of incorporating the collected images into a multimedia presentation on food webs. On the following visit to the library the students use the digital images and supportive text to create multimedia projects demonstrating the elements of a food web and the relationships between elements.

CONNECTION TO LOCAL OR STATE STANDARDS:

Content Standards for Grade 4 Science: Illustrate and explain the relationships among producers, consumers, and decomposers in a food web.

Content Standards for Grade 4 Educational Technology: Use technology tools (for example, multimedia authoring, presentation, web tools, digital cameras, scanners) for individual and collaborative writing, communication, and publishing activities to create knowledge products for audiences inside and outside the classroom.

OVERVIEW:

As a connection to a unit on ecology, fourth-grade students are given the opportunity to create multimedia projects in which they use digital images and text to illustrate food webs. The essential question is: How do food webs work?

FINAL PRODUCT:

Multimedia presentation

LIBRARY LESSONS:

Students will learn how to use a multimedia software application to create a presentation on food webs. Students will use library resources as necessary for reference.

ASSESSMENT

Product: Teacher, SLMS, and students use an SLMS-created rubric to assess the multimedia presentation on some of the following general criteria: content accuracy, organization, visuals, and format.

Process: Students complete exit passes at the end of each session to briefly describe progress, as well as problems they may be encountering.

Student self-questioning:

- What technology tools will help me organize and make sense of my information?
- Do I have enough information to prepare my presentation?
- What new understandings did I develop about the topic or idea?

INSTRUCTIONAL PLAN

Resources students will use:

- ■ Online subscription database(s)
- ■ Websites
- ■ Books
- ☐ Reference
- ■ Nonprint
- ☐ Periodicals/newspapers
- ■ Other (list): digital cameras, Kidspiration® software

INSTRUCTION/ACTIVITIES

Direct Instruction: The SLMS will provide instruction in the use of digital cameras, transferring images from the camera to the computer, and using Kidspiration® software to create a multimedia presentation.

Modeling and guided practice: Students will use digital cameras to collect images that will show parts of a food chain. They will explore and practice using the features of Kidspiration® software.

Independent practice: Students will use digital images and software to create a multimedia presentation and use library resources to create supportive text for the presentation.

Sharing and reflecting: Students will share multimedia presentations in a gallery walk and complete a self-evaluation rubric.

ACTION EXAMPLE: GRADE 5

GRADE: 5

LIBRARY CONTEXT:

- ■ Fixed
- ☐ Flexible
- ☐ Combination
- ☐ Individualized instruction
- ☐ Stand-alone lesson
- ■ Lesson in a unit
- ☐ Multiple lessons in a unit

COLLABORATION CONTINUUM:

- ☐ None
- ☐ Limited
- ☐ Moderate
- ■ Intensive

CONTENT TOPIC:

Nutritional Value of Snack Food

ESTIMATED LESSON TIME:

30 minutes

Standards for the 21st-Century Learner Goals

STANDARD 1: Inquire, think critically and gain knowledge.

SKILLS INDICATOR:

1.1.3   Develop and refine a range of questions to frame the search for new understanding.

BENCHMARKS:

– With guidance formulate questions about the topic.

– Assess questions to determine which can be answered by simple facts, which cannot be answered, and which would lead to an interesting inquiry.

DISPOSITIONS INDICATOR:

1.2.1   Display initiative and engagement by posing questions and investigating answers beyond the collection of superficial facts.

RESPONSIBILITIES INDICATOR:

NA

SELF-ASSESSMENT STRATEGIES INDICATORS:

2.4.2   Reflect on systematic process, and assess for completeness of investigation.

3.4.2   Assess the quality and effectiveness of the learning product.

SCENARIO:

The SLMS attends a meeting of fifth-grade teachers who discuss the annual Health Fair in which their students will focus on nutrition. The teachers want students to find information that goes beyond basic facts. The SLMS suggests a lesson for the students' next weekly forty-minute library visit in which they will learn how to construct higher-level questions. The team decides that the students will produce a brochure about healthy snacks. Together the teachers and the SLMS determine criteria for the brochure and split responsibilities. The teachers will introduce the unit and provide background information in the classroom; the SLMS will develop a lesson on questioning and a chart for students to record their questions. Subsequently, the teachers will continue instruction on this topic in their classrooms, and in a later lesson the SLMS will guide students through the process of selecting and using appropriate resources.

CONNECTION TO LOCAL OR STATE STANDARDS:

Content Standards for Grade 5 Health: The student can explain the importance of a healthy diet as part of a healthy lifestyle.

Content Standards for Grade 5 Language Arts: The student can conduct research by using effective questioning.

OVERVIEW:

Fifth-grade students investigate the nutritional value of foods; specifically students will determine which snack foods are healthiest and prepare a brochure based on their research for the school health fair.

FINAL PRODUCT:

Students create sets of basic and higher-level questions in preparation for designing and producing information brochures to distribute at the school health fair.

LIBRARY LESSON(S):

Students will identify the characteristics of higher-level questions. They will generate meaningful questions about the nutritional value of snack foods by creating a question chart that includes two columns: (1) factual questions and (2) higher-level questions.

ASSESSMENT

Product: Teachers, the SLMS, and students assess questions generated by the students to confirm that higher-level, as well as basic questions, have been generated in preparation for creating brochures intended for publication to a wider audience.

Process: Teachers and SLMS use the question charts generated by students to determine (1) whether student pairs correctly identified higher-level, as well as factual questions and (2) whether all questions were relevant to the topic of snack foods.

Student self-questioning:

– Did I show initiative by asking original questions?

– Did I ask questions that went beyond basic information?

– Will my questions lead me to find the information I need to produce an effective brochure?

INSTRUCTIONAL PLAN

Resources students will use:

☐ Online subscription database(s)

☐ Websites

☐ Books

☐ Reference

☐ Nonprint

☐ Periodicals/newspapers

■ Other (list): Question chart

INSTRUCTION/ACTIVITIES

Direct Instruction: Engage interest by sharing a display of different popular snack foods. Challenge students with the following questions: If you were to select the healthiest of these snack foods, which two would you pick? How would you know which are the healthiest?

Modeling and guided practice: Discuss the types of questions students might ask. Distinguish between factual questions and higher-order levels of questions. Use a matrix with examples of both types of questions.

Independent practice: Students work in pairs to create question charts with two columns headed "Basic Questions" and "Higher-Level Questions."

Sharing and reflecting: If time permits in the library (or if the classroom teachers are willing to continue the activity in the classroom), have students exchange their charts with another pair to discern the similarities and differences of their questions.

STRAND 1.1: SKILLS

STANDARD 1: Inquire, think critically and gain knowledge.

INDICATOR 1.1.1:

Follow an inquiry-based process in seeking knowledge in curricular subjects, and make the real-world connection for using this process in own life.

– Use a critical-thinking process that involves asking questions, investigating the answers, and developing new understandings for personal or academic independent-learning activities.

INDICATOR 1.1.2:

Use prior and background knowledge as context for new learning.

– State and support what is known about a topic, problem, or question, and make connections to prior knowledge.

– Observe and analyze an experience, demonstration, or source that introduces a topic, problem, or question to gather background information.

INDICATOR 1.1.3:

Develop and refine a range of questions to frame the search for new understanding.

– Write questions independently based on key ideas or areas of focus.

– Determine what information is needed to support the investigation and answer the questions.

– Analyze what is already known or what is observed or experienced to predict answers to inquiry questions.

– Refine questions depending on the type of information needed (for example, overview, big idea, specific detail, cause and effect, comparison).

INDICATOR 1.1.4:

Find, evaluate, and select appropriate sources to answer questions.

– Recognize the organization and use of special sections in the library (for example, reference, reserve books, paperbacks).

– Locate appropriate nonfiction resources by using the library's classification scheme.

– Evaluate sources based on criteria such as copyright date, authority of author or publisher, comprehensiveness, readability, and alignment with research needs.

– Select a variety of credible sources in different formats relevant to research needs.

INDICATOR 1.1.5:

Evaluate information found in selected sources on the basis of accuracy, validity, appropriateness for needs, importance, and social and cultural context.

– Recognize that information has a social or cultural context based on currency, accuracy, authority, and point of view.

– Evaluate and select information based on usefulness, currency, accuracy, authority, and point of view.

INDICATOR 1.1.6:

Read, view, and listen for information presented in any format (e.g., textual, visual, media, digital) in order to make inferences and gather meaning.

– Evaluate, paraphrase, and summarize information in various formats.

– Use both facts and opinions responsibly by identifying and verifying them.

INDICATOR 1.1.7: Make sense of information gathered from diverse sources by identifying misconceptions, main and supporting ideas, conflicting information, and point of view or bias.

– Seek more than one point of view by using diverse sources.

– Explain the effect of different perspectives (points of view) on the information.

INDICATOR 1.1.8: Demonstrate mastery of technology tools for accessing information and pursuing inquiry.

– Use technology resources, such as online encyclopedias, online databases, and Web subject directories, to locate information.

– Implement keyword search strategies.

– Select and use grade-level-appropriate electronic reference materials and teacher-selected websites to answer questions.

– Use a variety of search engines to do advanced searching.

INDICATOR 1.1.9: Collaborate with others to broaden and deepen understanding.

– Work in self-managed teams to understand concepts and to solve problems.

– Offer information and opinion at appropriate times in group discussions.

– Encourage team members to share ideas and opinions.

STRAND 2.1: SKILLS

STANDARD 2: Draw conclusions, make informed decisions, apply knowledge to new situations, and create new knowledge.

INDICATOR 2.1.1: Continue an inquiry-based research process by applying critical-thinking skills (analysis, synthesis, evaluation, organization) to information and knowledge in order to construct new understandings, draw conclusions, and create new knowledge.

– Assess the importance of ideas by comparing their treatment across texts.

– Identify main ideas and find supporting examples, definitions, and details.

– Analyze different points of view discovered in different sources.

– Determine patterns and discrepancies by comparing and combining information available in different sources.

– Interpret information and ideas by defining, classifying, and inferring from information in text.

INDICATOR 2.1.2: Organize knowledge so that it is useful.

– Combine and categorize information by using an outline or semantic web to find connections among ideas.

– Use common organizational patterns (chronological order, cause and effect, compare/contrast) to organize information and draw conclusions.

INDICATOR 2.1.3: Use strategies to draw conclusions from information and apply knowledge to curricular areas, real-world situations, and further investigations.

– Review prior knowledge and reflect on how ideas changed with more information.

– Compare information found to tentative thesis or hypothesis; revisit or revise hypothesis as appropriate.

– Draw conclusions based on explicit and implied information.

– Form opinions and judgments backed up by supporting evidence.

(continues on page 88)

(continued from page 87)

INDICATOR 2.1.4: Use technology and other information tools to analyze and organize information.

– Identify and apply common productivity tools and features such as menus and toolbars to plan, create, and edit word processing documents, spreadsheets, and presentations.

– Use interactive tools to participate as a group in analyzing and organizing information.

INDICATOR 2.1.5: Collaborate with others to exchange ideas, develop new understandings, make decisions, and solve problems.

– Participate in problem-solving process with group.

– Work collaboratively in using technology to meet information needs.

– Paying attention to copyright provisions, work in groups to import and manipulate pictures, images, and charts in documents, spreadsheets, presentations, webpages, and other creative products and presentations that effectively communicate new knowledge.

– Work in groups to evaluate products and presentations.

INDICATOR 2.1.6: Use the writing process, media and visual literacy, and technology skills to create products that express new understandings.

– Use prewriting to discover alternate ways to present conclusions.

– Select presentation form based on audience and purpose.

– Draft the presentation/product following an outline of ideas and add supporting details.

– Create products that incorporate writing, visuals, and other forms of media to convey message and main points.

– Assess and edit for grammar, visual impact, and appropriate use of media.

– Cite all sources using correct bibliographic format.

STRAND 3.1: SKILLS

STANDARD 3: Share knowledge and participate ethically and productively as members of our democratic society.

INDICATOR 3.1.1: Conclude an inquiry-based research process by sharing new understandings and reflecting on the learning.

– Present conclusions and supporting facts in a variety of ways.

– Present solutions to problems using modeled examples.

– Identify, with guidance, skills that require practice and refinement.

– Follow plan of work but seek feedback for improving the process.

– Reflect at the end of an inquiry process to identify additional areas of personal interest for pursuit in the future.

INDICATOR 3.1.2: Participate and collaborate as members of a social and intellectual network of learners.

– Offer information and opinions at appropriate times in group discussions.

– Encourage team members to share ideas and opinions.

– Ask questions of others in a group to elicit their information and opinions.

– Accurately describe or summarize ideas of others.

– Practice responsible and ethical use of information resources, both in their own library and in other institutions.

– Share reading experiences and favorite literature to build a relationship with others.

– Use interactive tools to exchange data collected, collaborate to design products or solve problems, and learn curricular concepts by communicating with peers, experts, and other audiences.

INDICATOR 3.1.3:

Use writing and speaking skills to communicate new understandings effectively.

- Present conclusions so that main ideas are clearly stated and supported by evidence.
- Use relevant ideas and details to show insight into people, events, new knowledge, and personal background.
- Use dramatic, audio, and video presentation as appropriate for subject and audience.
- Adjust pacing, volume, and intonation appropriate to content and purpose.

INDICATOR 3.1.4:

Use technology and other information tools to organize and display knowledge and understanding in ways that others can view, use, and assess.

- Use appropriate media and formats to design and develop products that clearly and coherently display new understanding.

INDICATOR 3.1.5:

Connect learning to community issues.

- Identify and address community and global issues.
- Use real-world examples to establish authenticity.
- Seek information from different sources to get balanced points of view.
- Articulate the importance of intellectual freedom to a democratic society.

INDICATOR 3.1.6:

Use information and technology ethically and responsibly.

- Avoid plagiarism by rephrasing information in their own words.
- Document quotations and cite sources using correct bibliographic format.
- Abide by Acceptable Use Policy by accessing only appropriate information.
- Use programs and websites responsibly and ethically.

STRAND 4.1: SKILLS

STANDARD 4: Pursue personal and aesthetic growth.

INDICATOR 4.1.1:

Read, view, and listen for pleasure and personal growth.

- Read, listen to, and view an increasingly wide range of genres and formats for recreation and information.
- Independently locate and select information for personal, hobby, or vocational interests.
- Pursue creative expressions of information in the community (public library, arts centers, museums).

INDICATOR 4.1.2:

Read widely and fluently to make connections with self, the world, and previous reading.

- Read books that connect to their own experiences.
- Read with purpose to investigate new ideas beyond the required curriculum.
- Read books from various genres.
- Compare and contrast story elements in two literary works.
- Demonstrate understanding that texts, both narrative and expository, are written by authors expressing their own ideas.
- Recognize the author's point of view; consider alternative perspectives.

INDICATOR 4.1.3:

Respond to literature and creative expressions of ideas in various formats and genres.

- Respond to the images and feelings evoked by a literary or artistic work.
- Connect text to personal experiences.

(continues on page 90)

(continued from page 89)

– Use illustrations, context, graphics, and layout to extract meaning from different formats.

– Interpret literary elements (plot, setting, characters, time) from evidence presented in the text.

– Draw conclusions about the theme from evidence in the text.

– Recognize how characters change.

– Share reading, listening, and viewing experiences in a variety of ways and formats.

INDICATOR 4.1.4:   **Seek information for personal learning in a variety of formats and genres.**

– Read a variety of genres, including short stories, novels, poems, plays, myths, films, and electronic magazines and books.

– Describe the characteristics of different genres.

– Explore new genres that fulfill interests and reading level (graphic novels, magazines, online magazines, e-books).

– Select resources for classroom learning and for personal exploration.

– Select resources on topics of interest at both a comfortable reading level and at higher levels of comprehension.

– Select print, nonprint, and electronic materials based on personal interests and knowledge of authors.

– Maintain personal reading lists.

INDICATOR 4.1.5:   **Connect ideas to own interests and previous knowledge and experience.**

– Demonstrate understanding of literal and implied meanings by explaining how new meanings fit with what is already known.

– Connect ideas reflected in various resources to life experiences at home, in school, and with peers.

– Keep a log or record of new and up-to-date ideas by reading online information, magazines, and other current sources.

– Check the ideas for accuracy by analyzing the authority of the source and validating the information through multiple resources.

INDICATOR 4.1.6:   **Organize personal knowledge in a way that can be called upon easily.**

– Develop visual pictures of the main ideas and design a concept maps, webs, or graphics to capture the ideas.

– Identify their own learning styles and organize ideas accordingly (for example, linear, graphic).

– Use different forms of note taking to capture personal connections to information.

INDICATOR 4.1.7:   **Use social networks and information tools to gather and share information.**

– Use advanced strategies (Boolean searches) to locate information about personal-interest topics in the library's online catalog.

– Use a few technology tools and resources to collect, organize, and evaluate information that addresses issues or interests.

– Apply technology productivity tools to meet personal needs.

– Use social networking tools to responsibly and safely share information and ideas, and to collaborate with others.

INDICATOR 4.1.8:   **Use creative and artistic formats to express personal learning.**

– Create original products based on responses to literature and other creative works of art.

– Experiment with various types of multimedia software for artistic and personal expression.

C.1 ACTION EXAMPLE: GRADE 6

LIBRARY CONTEXT:

- ☐ Fixed
- ■ Flexible
- ☐ Combination
- ☐ Individualized instruction
- ☐ Stand-alone lesson
- ☐ Lesson in a unit
- ■ Multiple lessons in a unit

COLLABORATION CONTINUUM:

- ☐ None
- ☐ Limited
- ☐ Moderate
- ■ Intensive

CONTENT TOPIC:

Obtaining and using natural resources and environmental impact of these actions

ESTIMATED LESSON TIME:

Two 50-minute library periods

Standards for the 21st Century Learner Goals

STANDARD 3: Share knowledge and participate ethically and productively as members of our democratic society.

SKILLS INDICATOR:

3.1.5 Connect learning to community issues.

BENCHMARKS:

- Identify and address community and global issues.
- Use real-world examples to establish authenticity.
- Seek information from different sources to get balanced points of view.

DISPOSITIONS INDICATOR:

2.2.4 Demonstrate personal productivity by completing products to express learning.

RESPONSIBILITIES INDICATOR:

2.3.1 Connect understanding to the real world.

SELF-ASSESSMENT STRATEGIES INDICATOR:

4.4.5 Develop personal criteria for gauging how effectively own ideas are expressed.

SCENARIO:

As part of the planning process for an upcoming sixth-grade science unit on sustainability the content leader for science makes an appointment with the SLMS. The content leader wants the students to engage in a research activity that will help them work with the content of the unit and connect to global issues. Together the content leader and the SLMS plan a series of lessons in which the students will research the impact on the environment of the acquisition and use of energy sources. Students will spend two periods doing research. The team decides that the students will participate in a mock panel discussion on the topic of alternative energy sources. Together the content leader and the SLMS create a rubric for the student research process and panel discussion. The science teacher will introduce the students to an overview of alternative energy sources before the visit to the library. Students will be divided into teams of two. The SLMS will guide students in the research process, note taking, creating citations, and the selection of resources.

CONNECTION TO LOCAL OR STATE STANDARDS:

Content Standards for Grade 6 Science: The student can explain how methods for obtaining and using resources such as water, minerals, and fossil fuel have consequences on the environment.

OVERVIEW:

As part of a science unit on conservation, sixth-grade students will research alternative energy sources and communicate their knowledge by participating in a mock panel discussion on alternative energy solutions. An essential question framing their inquiry is: Which alternative energy sources will sustain a healthier and cleaner environment?

FINAL PRODUCT:

Students compose prepared remarks and deliver oral presentations for panel discussions. All work must be properly cited.

LIBRARY LESSON:

Students will find and balance diverse points of view while researching a topic and citing their sources.

ASSESSMENT

Product: Teachers, the SLMS, and students use an instructor-designed rubric to assess the panel presentation on the basis of (1) content accuracy, (2) organization of ideas and details, and (3) communication skills.

Process: Teachers and the SLMS gauge student performance by using a rubric to assess students' progress in (1) generating and answering questions, (2) determining accuracy, credibility, and relevance of information (3) gathering information from appropriate sources, (4) taking notes in their own words, and (5) synthesizing notes for the presentation.

Student self-questioning:
– What are the sources that might be used?
– How do I locate these sources?
– Have I located sources with diverse perspectives?
– How well did my inquiry process go?

INSTRUCTIONAL PLAN

Resources students will use:
- ■ Online subscription database(s)
- ■ Websites
- ■ Books
- ■ Reference
- ■ Nonprint
- ■ Periodicals/newspapers
- ☐ Other (list)

INSTRUCTION/ACTIVITIES

Direct Instruction: The SLMS shares the book, *The True Story of the Three Little Pigs*, by A. Wolf, and facilitates a discussion in which the students identify the point of view of the pigs and the wolf.

Modeling and guided practice: The SLMS activates prior knowledge by asking the students to generate lists of energy sources. Students expand the list by brainstorming possible points of view in regard to each energy source. Each student chooses one alternative energy source to research. The SLMS demonstrates several information sources that represent diverse points of view on the topic and works with the students to identify search strategies appropriate for finding experts and sources.

Independent practice: Students gather information from a variety of sources and sort information to represent their selected energy sources.

Sharing and reflecting: Students participate in the mock panel discussion and complete a research process self-evaluation.

C.2 ACTION EXAMPLE: GRADE 7

LIBRARY CONTEXT:

☐ Fixed
■ Flexible
☐ Combination
☐ Individualized instruction
☐ Stand-alone lesson
☐ Lesson in a unit
■ Multiple lessons in a unit

COLLABORATION CONTINUUM:

☐ None
☐ Limited
☐ Moderate
■ Intensive

CONTENT TOPIC:

Community History

ESTIMATED LESSON TIME:

Six sessions, 45–60 minutes each

Standards for the 21st-Century Learner Goals

STANDARD 1: Inquire, think critically, and gain knowledge.

SKILLS INDICATORS:

1.1.4   Find, evaluate, and select appropriate sources to answer questions.

1.1.5   Evaluate information found in selected sources on the basis of accuracy, validity, appropriateness for needs, importance, and social and cultural context.

BENCHMARKS:

– Locate appropriate nonfiction resources by using the library's classification scheme.

– Evaluate sources based on criteria such as copyright date, authority of author or publisher, comprehensiveness, readability, and alignment with research needs.

– Select a variety of credible sources in different formats relevant to research needs.

– Evaluate and select information based on usefulness, currency, accuracy, authority, and point of view.

DISPOSITIONS INDICATORS:

1.2.1   Display initiative and engagement by posing questions and investigating answers beyond the collection of superficial facts.

1.2.4   Maintain a critical stance by questioning the validity and accuracy of all information.

RESPONSIBILITIES INDICATOR:

1.3.3   Follow ethical and legal guidelines in gathering and using information.

SELF-ASSESSMENT STRATEGIES INDICATORS:

1.4.1   Monitor own information-seeking processes for effectiveness and progress, and adapt as necessary.

1.4.3   Monitor gathered information, and assess for gaps or weaknesses.

SCENARIO:

Seventh-grade students in social studies focus on the history of their state as part of the grade-level curriculum. The social studies teachers decide that one way to pique students' curiosity about the state's past would be to start with the students' own community. They approach the SLMS with the concept of research on local history. She sparks excitement when she immediately agrees to involve the neighborhood public librarian and the regional archivist in this project. As a planning team, the teachers and SLMS decide that students might not only examine print, nonprint, and digital resources, but that this would be a great opportunity to teach students interview techniques. Toward this end, the SLMS also identifies potential human resources in the community, who can provide first-hand information about changes that have occurred in the community. This particular project extends over two months.

CONNECTION TO LOCAL OR STATE STANDARDS:

Content Standards for Grade 7 Social Studies: The student can analyze both change and continuity, and cause and/or effect in history.

Content Standards for Grade 7 Language Arts: The student can use a variety of grade-appropriate sources to research an inquiry question.

Content Standards for Grade 7 Technology: The student can demonstrate creative thinking and construct knowledge using technology.

OVERVIEW:

Seventh-grade students conduct a community history investigation that centers on the essential questions: How has our community changed over time? What caused or influenced these changes? How can we find out?

FINAL PRODUCT:

Students work in pairs to compose multimedia presentations that synthesize the information they have gleaned from readings, viewings, and interviews. The presentations are added to an online archive of student-produced materials on local history that the SLMS creates for the school.

LIBRARY LESSONS:

Students work with the SLMS in a series of six sessions focusing on various aspects of information gathering, including how to retrieve information from archival photographs, how to take notes from primary documents, how to conduct and analyze interviews, and how to properly cite these various resources.

ASSESSMENT

Product: Teachers, the SLMS, and students use a rubric created by the instructional team to critique the multimedia presentations that are the final product. The rubric includes criteria on content accuracy, organization, visual layout, and cited authority.

Process: Students maintain a running reflection log on their progress throughout the project. Some of the questions framing their entries are listed below under self-questioning.

Student self-questioning:

– What background information would help me get an overview of my topic so that I can ask good questions and learn more about it?

– What intriguing questions do I have about this topic?

– What is my plan for research?

– What are all the sources that might be used?

– How do I evaluate the information that I find?

– Have I found enough accurate information to answer all my questions?

– What new understandings did I develop about the topic?

INSTRUCTIONAL PLAN

Resources students will use:

☐ Online subscription database(s)

■ Websites

■ Books

■ Reference

■ Nonprint:

■ Periodicals/newspapers

■ Other (list): Primary documents, interviews

INSTRUCTION/ACTIVITIES

Note: These particular sessions focus on conducting an interview and how to assess an interview.

Direct Instruction: Introduce the interview as an important source of primary information for this particular research project. Go over an SLMS-designed checklist of pre-interview, interview, and post-interview steps. The steps might include the following: stating goals, gathering sufficient background information on topic, setting up the interview, preparing and sequencing the questions, rehearsing, and practicing appropriate interview etiquette.

Modeling and guided practice: Have the SLMS and teacher model a mock interview being conducted. Invite the students to use the portion of the checklist that focuses on how to conduct an interview as they observe the SLMS and teacher perform. Critique the interview together.

Independent practice: This portion must be done by the students in the actual interviews. The SLMS assists with scheduling since the interviewees are invited to the school library where the interviews are conducted.

Sharing and reflecting: In a session after the actual interviews have been conducted, have students focus on an assessment of the interviews. Questions might focus on completeness of information gleaned, possible conflicts between the interviewee's comments and information gathered from other sources, and strategies to resolve any conflicts and fill gaps in information.

ACTION EXAMPLE: GRADE 8

GRADE: 8

LIBRARY CONTEXT:

- ☐ Fixed
- ☐ Flexible
- ■ Combination
- ☐ Individualized instruction
- ☐ Stand-alone lesson
- ☐ Lesson in a unit
- ■ Multiple lessons in a unit

COLLABORATION CONTINUUM:

- ☐ None
- ☐ Limited
- ■ Moderate
- ☐ Intensive

CONTENT TOPIC:

Global Warming

ESTIMATED LESSON TIME:

Three to five 50-minute sessions in the library with individual follow-up as students finalize projects.

Standards for the 21st-Century Learner Goals

STANDARD 3: Share knowledge and participate ethically and productively as members of our democratic society.

SKILLS INDICATORS:

3.1.4 Use technology and other information tools to organize and display knowledge and understanding in ways that others can view, use, and assess.

3.1.6 Use information and technology ethically and responsibly.

BENCHMARK(S):

- Use appropriate media and formats to design and develop products that clearly and coherently display new understanding.
- Avoid plagiarism by rephrasing information in their own words.
- Document quotations and cite sources using correct bibliographic format.
- Abide by Acceptable Use Policy by accessing only appropriate information.
- Use programs and websites responsibly and ethically.

DISPOSITIONS INDICATOR(S):

2.2.4 Demonstrate personal productivity by completing products to express learning.

3.2.1 Demonstrate leadership and confidence by presenting ideas to others in both formal and informal situations.

RESPONSIBILITIES INDICATOR(S):

3.3.5 Contribute to the exchange of ideas within and beyond the learning community.

3.3.7 Respect the principles of intellectual freedom.

SELF-ASSESSMENT STRATEGIES INDICATOR(S):

1.4.1 Monitor own information-seeking processes for effectiveness and progress, and adapt as necessary.

3.4.2 Assess the quality and effectiveness of the learning product.

In an integrated science/math/language arts unit, eighth-grade students are working on individual investigations of a topic related to global warming. Each student is required to create an electronic portfolio that illustrates key information related to that topic. Students will present their portfolios at the end of the school year at an evening open house for parents, faculty, and community members in the library media center. Several students will be presenting simultaneously with opportunities for the audience to ask questions of each student. The eighth-grade teaching team has asked the SLMS to assist the language arts teacher in teaching the students how to create an annotated "works cited" list using an online citation generator. The SLMS has team-taught lessons on intellectual property and information processing with the language arts teacher during the course of the project. The SLMS has also worked with individual students to identify essential citation information for the various resources they have collected. Because the students will present their portfolios in the library, each student will have a rehearsal in the library with the SLMS and the eighth-grade teaching team before the open house.

CONNECTION TO LOCAL OR STATE STANDARDS:

Content Standards for Grade 8 Information Literacy: The student can locate sources, use information, and present findings.

Content Standards for Grade 8 Math: The student can demonstrate understanding of an ability to use data analysis, probability, and statistics.

Content Standards for Grade 8 Science: The student can demonstrate knowledge of the composition, structures, processes, and interactions of Earth's systems and other objects in space.

Content Standards for Grade 8 Technology: The student can apply digital tools and skills with creativity and innovation to express himself/herself, construct knowledge, and develop products and processes.

OVERVIEW:

Eighth-grade students will synthesize learning in science, mathematics, and language arts to present accurate, relevant, authoritative, and current information about global warming using digital tools and information-processing strategies. The essential questions are: Has the climate of our world changed in the last fifty years because of human activity? How can you justify your response?

FINAL PRODUCT:

The student develops a portfolio that will contain: photographs/illustrations, graphs/charts, vocabulary list, a student-generated podcast, and an annotated "works cited" list of current resources.

LIBRARY LESSONS:

Students will learn: how to identify project-appropriate resources, how to effectively use a range of resources, how to define and identify intellectual property, and how to ethically credit the owners of intellectual property.

ASSESSMENT

Product: The eighth-grade team, SLMS, and students use an instructor-designed rubric for each required portion of the portfolio and presentation. General criteria used for the portfolio include: statements of objectives, samples of products/performance aligned with the objectives, and evaluations and student reflections on the quality of work. The annotated list of works cited will conform to MLA formatting and include all elements of an annotation as taught.

Process: Students will maintain a self-assessment journal throughout their work on this project based on the student self-assessment questions below.

Student self-questioning:

- Have I completed each required portion of this assignment to the best of my ability?
- Have I followed the rules for accessing information and technology?
- Have I credited each source of information in the correct format?
- Have I adequately described each source in the annotated works cited list?
- Have I adequately answered the essential questions for this project?

INSTRUCTIONAL PLAN

Resources students will use:

- Online subscription database(s)
- Websites
- Books
- Reference
- Nonprint
- Periodicals/newspapers
- Other (list): photos, video clips

INSTRUCTION/ACTIVITIES

Note: These particular sessions focus on citing sources and assessing the learning process.

Direct Instruction: The SLMS will instruct the students on MLA rules for citing sources and provide example "formulas" in a mini style sheet to help students generate "works cited" entries for their own project resources. The SLMS will give instructions on how to access the online citation generator (usernames/passwords, URL, etc.). The SLMS will define an annotated list of works cited and provide examples of annotations. The model annotations will include: a brief statement about the format and topic, the author/creator's credentials, three significant facts learned from the source, and a statement about why the source was chosen.

Modeling and guided practice: The SLMS will use student project resources to create two or three sample MLA citations with the class. For several format examples the SLMS will demonstrate data entry in the online citation generator and will guide students through one or two examples generated from the class. After writing a model annotation with the whole class, the SLMS will guide individual students in writing concise and clear annotations for a variety of formats during the remainder of the lesson.

Independent practice: Students will independently complete MLA citations for each project resource using the mini style sheet. They will complete a generic form to transfer citation information from source cards before entering information into an online citation generator. Annotations for each of their sources will include a brief statement about the format and topic, the author/creator's credentials, three significant facts learned from the source, and a statement about why the source was chosen.

Sharing and reflecting: After the final presentation, students will use a "3,2,1" model to talk about the project and their learning process. Each student will list three things learned, list two things to do differently for the next project, and write one burning question that was left unanswered. The students' work will be shared and preserved by including the portfolios in the library collection.

STRAND 1.1: SKILLS

STANDARD 1: Inquire, think critically and gain knowledge.

INDICATOR 1.1.1:

Follow an inquiry-based process in seeking knowledge in curricular subjects, and make the real-world connection for using this process in own life.

– With guidance, use an inquiry-based process for expanding content knowledge, connecting academic learning with the real world, and pursuing personal interests.

INDICATOR 1.1.2:

Use prior and background knowledge as context for new learning.

– Read background information to discover the key components of the problem or question.

– Identify keywords or synonyms to use in further research.

– Develop a schema or mind map to express the big idea and the relationships among supporting ideas and topics of interest.

INDICATOR 1.1.3:

Develop and refine a range of questions to frame the search for new understanding.

– Generate specific questions to focus the purpose of the research.

– Develop and refine the topic, problem, or question independently to arrive at a worthy and manageable topic.

– Formulate questions to collect the needed information to validate or contest a thesis statement.

– Design questions that systematically test a hypothesis or validate a thesis statement.

– Refine questions to provide a framework for the inquiry and to fulfill the purpose of the research.

INDICATOR 1.1.4:

Find, evaluate, and select appropriate sources to answer questions.

– Identify and prioritize possible sources of information based on specific information needs and strengths of different information formats.

– Use specialized reference materials to find specific and in-depth information.

– Use both primary and secondary sources.

– Evaluate sources based on criteria such as copyright date, authority of author or publisher, depth of coverage, and relevance to research questions.

INDICATOR 1.1.5:

Evaluate information found in selected sources on the basis of accuracy, validity, appropriateness for needs, importance, and social and cultural context.

– Recognize that knowledge can be organized into disciplines that influence the way information is presented and use this understanding to effectively access information.

– Evaluate information from a variety of social or cultural contexts, based on currency, accuracy, authority, and point of view.

INDICATOR 1.1.6:

Read, view, and listen for information presented in any format (e.g., textual, visual, media, digital) in order to make inferences and gather meaning.

– Take notes using one or more note-taking strategies, including reflecting on the information (for example, graphic organizers, two-column notes).

– Categorize information; add new categories as necessary.

– Interpret information presented in various formats.

INDICATOR 1.1.7:

Make sense of information gathered from diverse sources by identifying misconceptions, main and supporting ideas, conflicting information, and point of view or bias.

– Identify presence of bias and explain the effect on the information presented.

– Counter the effect of bias on the accuracy and reliability of information by actively pursuing a balanced perspective.

INDICATOR 1.1.8:

Demonstrate mastery of technology tools for accessing information and pursuing inquiry.

– Use a range of electronic resources efficiently, effectively, and safely by applying a variety of search and evaluation strategies.

– Use social networking tools to demonstrate and share learning.

INDICATOR 1.1.9:

Collaborate with others to broaden and deepen understanding.

– Seek ideas and opinions from others.

– Respect and help groups find and incorporate diverse ideas.

– Describe ideas of others accurately.

– Help to organize and integrate contributions of all group members in to products.

STRAND 2.1: SKILLS

STANDARD 2: Draw conclusions, make informed decisions, apply knowledge to new situations, and create new knowledge.

INDICATOR 2.1.1:

Continue an inquiry-based research process by applying critical-thinking skills (analysis, synthesis, evaluation, organization) to information and knowledge in order to construct new understandings, draw conclusions, and create new knowledge.

– Identify main, supporting, and conflicting information using multiple sources to support interpretation or point of view.

– Make and explain inferences about main ideas.

– Critically examine and analyze relevant information from a variety of sources to discover relationships and patterns among ideas.

– If a discrepancy in points of view is discovered, continue research until it is resolved.

INDICATOR 2.1.2:

Organize knowledge so that it is useful.

– Use appropriate organizational patterns (chronological order, cause and effect, compare/contrast) to capture point of view and draw conclusions.

– Experiment with devising their own organizational structures.

INDICATOR 2.1.3:

Use strategies to draw conclusions from information and apply knowledge to curricular areas, real-world situations, and further investigations.

– Draw clear and appropriate conclusions supported by evidence and examples.

– Combine ideas and information to develop and demonstrate new understanding.

– Recognize multiple causes for same issues or events.

– Apply strategies for making personal and real world connections with information.

INDICATOR 2.1.4:

Use technology and other information tools to analyze and organize information.

– Use web-based and other technology tools to show connections and patterns in the ideas and information collected.

99

(continues on page 100)

(continued from page 99)

– Identify and apply common utilities (for example, spellchecker and thesaurus for word processing; formulas and charts in spreadsheets; and pictures, movies, sound, and charts in presentation tools) to enhance communication to an audience, promote productivity, and support creativity.

INDICATOR 2.1.5: | **Collaborate with others to exchange ideas, develop new understandings, make decisions, and solve problems.**

– Participate in discussion to analyze information problems to suggest solutions.

– Work with others to select, organize, and integrate information and ideas from a variety of sources and formats.

– Use online environments or other collaborative tools to facilitate design and development of materials, models, publications, and presentations.

– Apply utilities to edit pictures, images, and charts, complying with all copyright provisions.

INDICATOR 2.1.6: | **Use the writing process, media and visual literacy, and technology skills to create products that express new understandings.**

– Select the presentation/product to effectively communicate and support a purpose, argument, point of view, or interpretation.

– Express ideas through creative products in a variety of formats.

– Revise work based on ongoing self-assessment and feedback from teachers and peers.

– Edit for grammar, language conventions, and style.

– Cite all sources and use specified citation formats.

STRAND 3.1: SKILLS

STANDARD 3: Share knowledge and participate ethically and productively as members of our democratic society.

INDICATOR 3.1.1: | **Conclude an inquiry-based research process by sharing new understandings and reflecting on the learning.**

– Present and support conclusions to answer the question or problem.

– Set high and clear standards for work and develop criteria for self-assessment or use established criteria (rubrics, checklists).

– Assess their own work and establish revision strategies for themselves.

– Follow their own research plans and evaluate effectiveness of their inquiry processes.

INDICATOR 3.1.2: | **Participate and collaborate as members of a social and intellectual network of learners.**

– Seek ideas and opinions from others.

– Respect and help groups find and incorporate diverse ideas.

– Accurately describe or summarize ideas of others and respond appropriately.

– Respect guidelines and comply with policies for access in different information environments (public libraries, museums, cultural institutions, agencies).

– Recognize that equitable access to information depends on student responsibility.

– Use interactive tools and websites to collaboratively design products and solve problems with peers, experts, and other audiences.

– Share research and creative products with others.

INDICATOR 3.1.3: Use writing and speaking skills to communicate new understandings effectively.

– Use an organizational structure that effectively connects ideas and creates the desired intent.

– Use the most appropriate format, tone, and language to communicate ideas and points of view clearly to different audiences.

INDICATOR 3.1.4: Use technology and other information tools to organize and display knowledge and understanding in ways that others can view, use, and assess.

– Use a variety of media and formats to communicate information and ideas effectively to multiple audiences.

INDICATOR 3.1.5: Connect learning to community issues.

– Use multiple resources to seek balanced perspectives.

– Explain how the topic or question relates to issues in the real world.

– Demonstrate understanding of intellectual freedom and First Amendment rights.

INDICATOR 3.1.6: Use information and technology ethically and responsibly.

– Understand what constitutes plagiarism and refrain from representing others' work attributable to as their own.

– Demonstrate understanding of intellectual property rights by giving credit for all quotes, and by citing them properly in notes and bibliography.

– Abide by copyright guidelines for use of materials not in public domain.

– Legally obtain, store, and disseminate text, data, images, or sounds.

– Abide by the acceptable use policy in all respects and use Internet responsibly and safely.

– Explain First Amendment rights and the process available to defend them.

STRAND 4.1: SKILLS

STANDARD 4: Pursue personal and aesthetic growth.

INDICATOR 4.1.1: Read, view, and listen for pleasure and personal growth.

– Read, listen to, and view information in a variety of formats to explore new ideas, form opinions, and solve problems.

– Seek and locate information about personal interests, applying the same criteria and strategies used for academic information seeking.

INDICATOR 4.1.2: Read widely and fluently to make connections with self, the world, and previous reading.

– Recognize and evaluate the author's point of view and how it affects the text; consider and evaluate alternative perspectives.

– Read books that connect to real-world issues.

– Recognize similarities and differences among authors writing on the same theme.

– Recognize how their own points of view influence perspectives on text.

INDICATOR 4.1.3: Respond to literature and creative expressions of ideas in various formats and genres.

– Assess the emotional impact of specific works on the reader or viewer.

– Apply ideas gained from literary and artistic works to their own lives.

– Compare the theme and its treatment in different works of literature.

– Evaluate the effectiveness of a creative work in terms of the creator's use and interweaving of artistic elements.

(continues on page 102)

(continued from page 101)

INDICATOR 4.1.4: **Seek information for personal learning in a variety of formats and genres.**

– Select resources for academic, personal, and real-world purposes.

– Select print, nonprint, and digital materials based on personal interests and knowledge of authors.

– Select resources on topics of interest at both comfortable and challenging levels of comprehension.

– Read a variety of fiction and nonfiction, including works of international authors and authors outside students' own cultures.

– Use print, nonprint, and electronic information resources for information about personal needs; actively seek answers to questions.

– Set reading goals and maintain personal reading lists.

INDICATOR 4.1.5: **Connect ideas to own interests and previous knowledge and experience.**

– Explain text on both literal and abstract levels.

– Use context and graphic clues to aid understanding.

– Analyze alternative perspectives and evaluate differing points of view.

– Compare new ideas to previous understandings and make changes to mental framework where appropriate.

INDICATOR 4.1.6: **Organize personal knowledge in a way that can be called upon easily.**

– Use visualization to provide a clear picture of the major ideas.

– Categorize new ideas with keywords and tagging.

– Develop personal note-taking systems that incorporate personal reflections.

INDICATOR 4.1.7: **Use social networks and information tools to gather and share information.**

– Expand use of technology tools and resources to collect, organize, and evaluate information that addresses issues or interests.

– Use a range of search strategies to locate information about personal-interest topics in their own and other libraries.

– Engage in safe and ethical use of social networking applications to construct and share ideas and products.

– Share reading, viewing, and listening experiences in a variety of ways and formats, including book clubs and interest groups.

INDICATOR 4.1.8: **Use creative and artistic formats to express personal learning.**

– Express their own ideas through creative products in a variety of formats.

– Choose format appropriate for audience and purpose.

– Select and use various types of multimedia software for artistic and personal expression.

ACTION EXAMPLE: GRADE 9

Standards for the 21st-Century Learner Goals

STANDARD 4: Pursue personal and aesthetic growth.

SKILLS INDICATOR:

4.1.7   Use social networks and information tools to gather and share information.

BENCHMARKS:

- Expand use of technology tools and resources to collect, organize, and evaluate information that addresses issues or interests.
- Use a range of search strategies to locate information about personal-interest topics in their own and other libraries.
- Engage in safe and ethical use of social networking applications to construct and share ideas and products.

DISPOSITIONS INDICATORS:

4.2.1   Display curiosity by pursuing interests through multiple resources.

4.2.2   Demonstrate motivation by seeking information to answer personal questions and interests, trying a variety of formats and genres, and displaying a willingness to go beyond academic requirements.

RESPONSIBILITIES INDICATORS:

4.3.1   Participate in the social exchange of ideas, both electronically and in person.

4.3.4   Practice safe and ethical behaviors in personal electronic communication and interaction.

SELF-ASSESSMENT STRATEGIES INDICATORS:

1.4.2   Use interaction with and feedback from teachers and peers to guide own inquiry process.

1.4.4   Seek appropriate help when it is needed.

4.4.1   Identify own areas of interest.

A ninth-grade student has recently completed a traditional research paper on her favorite author, Jane Austen. In a conversation with the SLMS, the student indicates that she would like to create a blog that includes information she gathered for her research paper and helps her connect with other fans of the author. The student would like to e-mail a Jane Austen scholar to ask questions but is not sure about protocol for e-mailing an expert. Upon further conversation, the SLMS encourages the student to bring her research paper to the SLMS for review of the paper and the "works cited" list. After reviewing the research paper and list of citations, the SLMS suggests that the student expand the resources used for the research paper to include a bibliography of Austen's novels and books written about the author's work, along with links to graphics, video and audio clips from Austen's novels. The SLMS also suggests that the student may want to create a wiki, rather than a blog, to better share information. The SLMS then meets with the ninth-grade team and proposes that a wiki would be a great addition to the research unit. The wiki would be a way to follow up and share what students learn from their research papers. The SLMS offers to teach wiki design as an additional element in the project.

CONNECTION TO LOCAL OR STATE STANDARDS:

Content Standard for Grade 9 Language Arts: The student can use the writing process and conventions of language and research to construct meaning and communicate effectively for a variety of purposes and audiences using a range of forms.

Content Standard for Grade 9 Information Literacy/Library Media Standard: The student can locate sources, use information, and present findings.

Content Standard for Grade 9 Information Literacy/Library Media Standard: The student can use information safely, ethically and legally.

Content Standard for Grade 9 Information Literacy/Library Media Standard: The student can pursue personal interests through literature and other creative expressions.

Content Standard for Grade 9 Technology: The student can pursue personal interests through literature and other creative expressions.

OVERVIEW:

The student wishes to share and expand upon information synthesized in an English I research assignment. In particular, the student wishes to exchange information with others interested in the same author.

FINAL PRODUCT:

The student designs a wiki that includes a variety of resources and a component for exchanging information with visitors to the wiki.

LIBRARY LESSONS:

The SLMS conducts informal, one-on-one instructional sessions and conferences with the student. These meetings focus on searches for additional resources, netiquette required for online exchanges, and methods to build and sustain learning through social networks.

ASSESSMENT

Product: The student and SLMS will create a self-assessment checklist to include criteria for (1) wiki design, (2) quality and variety of resources, (3) reliability and accuracy of information, and (4) appropriate credit for sources of information. The student and the SLMS will also use a SWOT (Strengths, Weakness, Opportunities and Threats) analysis to evaluate the wiki.

Process: Throughout her independent research the student will maintain a reflection log, based on the student self-assessment questions below, to share with the SLMS at their meetings.

Student self-questioning:
- Did I effectively expand the information beyond my original report?
- Did I gather good information from experts?
- Did I find new pictures, audio, or video to add to the original research?
- Did I achieve my goal to share my information with others outside of my class and school?
- Did I achieve my goal of connecting with other people who share my interest in Jane Austen?

INSTRUCTIONAL PLAN

Resources students will use:
- Online subscription database(s)
- Websites
- Books
- Reference
- Nonprint
- Periodicals/newspapers
- Other (list): Audio recordings, DVD movies, or other video sources

INSTRUCTION/ACTIVITIES

Direct Instruction: The SLMS reviews the online and library collection resources presented during the English I research project and suggests additional resources. The SLMS also reviews netiquette rules for safely and responsibly using electronic resources and for communicating using e-mail or other online communication tools, and provides instruction on how to choose a wiki site and how to set up the basic account information and design.

Modeling and guided practice: The SLMS works with the student to identify search strategies appropriate for finding experts and multimedia resources and assists the student in searching WorldCat for scholarly works on Jane Austen. The SLMS challenges the student to develop new questions that will lead to discovery of new information and understandings about the author and her works and guides the student toward examples of well-designed wikis.

Independent practice: The student uses independent time to search for resources and make contact with experts. She creates and implements a wiki design that includes appropriately credited content and links to multimedia resources.

Sharing and reflecting: The student and SLMS review the self-assessment checklist. The student completes a SWOT

D.2 ACTION EXAMPLE: GRADE 10

LIBRARY CONTEXT:

- ☐ Fixed
- ☐ Flexible
- ☐ Combination
- ☐ Individualized instruction
- ☐ Stand-alone lesson
- ☐ Lesson in a unit
- ☐ Multiple lessons in a unit

COLLABORATION CONTINUUM:

- ☐ None
- ☐ Limited
- ☐ Moderate
- ☐ Intensive

CONTENT TOPIC:

Using InspireData software to compare data

ESTIMATED LESSON TIME:

One 50-minute session

Standards for the 21st-Century Learner Goals

STANDARD 2: Draw conclusions, make informed decisions, apply knowledge to new situations, and create new knowledge.

SKILLS INDICATOR:

2.1.4 Use technology and other information tools to analyze and organize information.

BENCHMARKS:

- Use web-based and other technology tools to show connections and patterns in the ideas and information collected.
- Identify and apply common utilities (for example, spellchecker and thesaurus for word processing; formulas and charts in spreadsheets; and pictures, movies, sound, and charts in presentation tools) to enhance communication to an audience, promote productivity and support creativity.

DISPOSITIONS INDICATOR:

2.2.3 Employ a critical stance in drawing conclusions by demonstrating that the pattern of evidence leads to a decision or conclusion.

RESPONSIBILITIES INDICATOR:

3.3.4 Create products that apply to authentic, real-world contexts.

SELF-ASSESSMENT STRATEGIES INDICATOR:

1.4.3 Monitor gathered information, and assess for gaps or weaknesses.

SCENARIO:

The SLMS is approached by an algebra teacher who attended a professional development session where the SLMS demonstrated InspireData software that allows students to use a variety of charts and graphs to manipulate and analyze data. She wants the SLMS to teach her students how to use this software. The SLMS suggests that the lesson will be more effective if the students actually have data to input. They schedule the teacher's six classes in the library computer lab one at a time for a 50-minute lesson on use of the InspireData application. The teacher decides that students will plan a trip to Chicago. As part of that planning, they must decide on the best mode of transportation based on the cost of travel and the amount of time required by that particular mode. The students will use predetermined websites to collect costs and times needed to travel by train, car, bus, and plane. Once they have collected their data, they will receive instruction on the use of the InspireData software. The SLMS will guide the students through the features of the software at which time they will input their data. They take their printed graphs with their data back to math class for review, presentation, and assessment.

CONNECTION TO LOCAL OR STATE STANDARDS:

Content Standards for Grade 10 Algebra: The student can use two or more types of graphs to compare data sets.

OVERVIEW:

Tenth-grade algebra students gather data, manipulate the data, and then examine and manipulate various types of graphs to determine the appropriateness of different graphs in relation to the data.

FINAL PRODUCT:

Students produce graphs comparing cost and time of various modes of transportation.

LIBRARY LESSON:

Students will learn to use the features of the InspireData application and explore the various types of graphs that can be made using the software. Students will use data collected about the cost and time required to get from their hometown to Chicago using several modes of transportation. In the process learners analyze how best to graph the data depending on the intended purpose.

ASSESSMENT

Product: Teacher, SLMS, and students use a teacher-developed rubric to assess the graphs based on the appropriate choice of graph type in relation to information collected, as well as reaching a conclusion based on analysis of data.

Process: Teacher and SLMS use the graphs generated by the students to determine whether students can use the software correctly.

Student self-questioning:

– Is my choice of the best mode of transportation supported by the evidence?

– Have I chosen the most appropriate type of graph to show my conclusion?

INSTRUCTIONAL PLAN

Resources students will use:

☐ Online subscription database(s)

■ Websites

☐ Books

☐ Reference

☐ Nonprint

☐ Periodicals/newspapers

■ Other (list): InspireData software

Websites:

<http://studenttravel.about.com>

<www.amtrak.com>

<www.aa.com>

<www.greyhound.com>

INSTRUCTION/ACTIVITIES

Direct Instruction: The SLMS introduces students to features of the InspireData software.

Modeling and guided practice: Using data gathered by the SLMS from the same websites that the students will use, students input the data along with the SLMS. They try manipulating the data with various types of graphs and decide as a class which one most effectively represents the data.

Independent practice: Students input the data they collected, choose the graph type that best compares their data and print their completed graph.

Sharing and reflecting: These graphs and conclusions will be shared and critiqued in the classroom.

SKILL BENCHMARKS TO ACHIEVE BY GRADE 12

STRAND 1.1: SKILLS

STANDARD 1: Inquire, think critically and gain knowledge.

INDICATOR 1.1.1:

Follow an inquiry-based process in seeking knowledge in curricular subjects, and make the real-world connection for using this process in own life.

- Independently and systematically use an inquiry-based process to deepen content knowledge, connect academic learning with the real world, pursue personal interests, and investigate opportunities for personal growth.

INDICATOR 1.1.2:

Use prior and background knowledge as context for new learning.

- Explore general information sources to increase familiarity with the topic or question.
- Review the initial information need to develop, clarify, revise, or refine the question.
- Compare new background information with prior knowledge to determine direction and focus of new learning.

INDICATOR 1.1.3:

Develop and refine a range of questions to frame the search for new understanding.

- Recognize that the purpose of the inquiry determines the type of questions and the type of thinking required (for example, an historical purpose may require taking a position and defending it).
- Explore problems or questions for which there are multiple answers or no "best" answer.
- Review the initial information need to clarify, revise, or refine the questions.

INDICATOR 1.1.4:

Find, evaluate, and select appropriate sources to answer questions.

- Identify the value of and differences among potential resources in a variety of formats.
- Use various search systems to retrieve information in a variety of formats.
- Seek and use a variety of specialized resources available from libraries, the Web, and the community.
- Describe criteria used to make resource decisions and choices.

INDICATOR 1.1.5:

Evaluate information found in selected sources on the basis of accuracy, validity, appropriateness for needs, importance, and social and cultural context.

- Evaluate historical information for validity of interpretation, and scientific information for accuracy and reliability of data.
- Recognize the social, cultural, or other context within which the information was created and explain the impact of context on interpreting the information.
- Use consciously selected criteria to determine whether the information contradicts or verifies information from other sources.

INDICATOR 1.1.6:

Read, view, and listen for information presented in any format (e.g., textual, visual, media, digital) in order to make inferences and gather meaning.

- Restate concepts in their own words and select appropriate data accurately.
- Integrate new information presented in various formats with previous information or knowledge.
- Analyze initial synthesis of findings and construct new hypotheses or generalizations if warranted.
- Challenge ideas represented and make notes of questions to pursue in additional sources.

INDICATOR 1.1.7: Make sense of information gathered from diverse sources by identifying misconceptions, main and supporting ideas, conflicting information, and point of view or bias.

- Create a system to organize the information.
- Analyze the structure and logic of supporting arguments or methods.
- Analyze information for prejudice, deception, or manipulation.
- Investigate different viewpoints encountered and determine whether and how to incorporate or reject these viewpoints.
- Compensate for the effect of point of view and bias by seeking alternative perspectives.

INDICATOR 1.1.8: Demonstrate mastery of technology tools for accessing information and pursuing inquiry.

- Select the most appropriate technologies to access and retrieve the needed information.
- Use various technologies to organize and manage the information selected.
- Create their own electronic learning spaces by collecting and organizing links to information resources, working collaboratively, and sharing new ideas and understandings with others.

INDICATOR 1.1.9: Collaborate with others to broaden and deepen understanding.

- Model social skills and character traits that advance a team's ability to identify issues and problems, and to work together on solutions and products.
- Design and implement projects that include participation from diverse groups.

STRAND 2.1: SKILLS

STANDARD 2: Draw conclusions, make informed decisions, apply knowledge to new situations, and create new knowledge.

INDICATOR 2.1.1: Continue an inquiry-based research process by applying critical-thinking skills (analysis, synthesis, evaluation, organization) to information and knowledge in order to construct new understandings, draw conclusions, and create new knowledge.

- Build a conceptual framework by synthesizing ideas gathered from multiple texts.
- Resolve conflicting evidence or clarify reasons for differing interpretations of information and ideas.

INDICATOR 2.1.2: Organize knowledge so that it is useful.

- Organize information independently, deciding the structure based on the relationships among ideas and general patterns discovered.

INDICATOR 2.1.3: Use strategies to draw conclusions from information and apply knowledge to curricular areas, real-world situations, and further investigations.

- Combine information and inferences to draw conclusions and create meaning.
- Develop their own points of view and support with evidence.
- Present different perspectives with evidence for each.
- Apply new knowledge to real-world issues and problems.

INDICATOR 2.1.4: Use technology and other information tools to analyze and organize information.

- Display important connections among ideas by using common productivity tools to categorize and analyze information.
- Use locally available and web-based interactive presentation and production tools to enhance creativity in effectively organizing and communicating information.

(continues on page 110)

(continued from page 109)

INDICATOR 2.1.5: Collaborate with others to exchange ideas, develop new understandings, make decisions, and solve problems.

– Collaborate locally and remotely with peers, experts, and others to collect, produce, and share information.

– Work with others to solve problems and make decisions on issues, topics, and themes being investigated.

INDICATOR 2.1.6: Use the writing process, media and visual literacy, and technology skills to create products that express new understandings.

– Use the most appropriate format to clearly communicate ideas to targeted audiences.

– Assess how tone and choice of language impact content in a range of media.

– Analyze how composition and placement of visual images influence the message.

– Apply various technological skills to create performances and products.

– Cite ideas and direct quotes using official style formats.

– Employ various strategies for revising and reviewing their own work.

STRAND 3.1: SKILLS

STANDARD 3: Share knowledge and participate ethically and productively as members of our democratic society.

INDICATOR 3.1.1: Conclude an inquiry-based research process by sharing new understandings and reflecting on the learning.

– Present complex ideas with clarity and authority.

– Present original conclusions effectively.

– Identify their own strengths, assess their own inquiry processes and products, and set goals for improvement.

INDICATOR 3.1.2: Participate and collaborate as members of a social and intellectual network of learners.

– Offer and defend information brought to group.

– Seek consensus from a group, when appropriate, to achieve a stronger product.

– Help to organize and integrate contributions of all group members into products.

– Use technology tools to collaborate, publish, and interact with peers, experts, and other real-world audiences.

INDICATOR 3.1.3: Use writing and speaking skills to communicate new understandings effectively.

– Employ organizational and presentation structures (for example, narrative essays, poems, debates) using various formats to achieve purpose and clarify meaning.

– Use details and language that show authority and knowledge of topic.

– Deliver a presentation to support a position on a specified topic and respond to questions from the audience.

– Present ideas and conclusions to audiences beyond the school.

INDICATOR 3.1.4: Use technology and other information tools to organize and display knowledge and understanding in ways that others can view, use, and assess.

– Prepare and deliver a "professional" presentation to audiences outside of school using technology as medium of presentation.

INDICATOR 3.1.5: **Connect learning to community issues.**

– Investigate multiple sides of issues and evaluate them carefully, particularly on controversial or culturally based topics.

– Connect learning to real-world issues.

INDICATOR 3.1.6: **Use information and technology ethically and responsibly.**

– Demonstrate understanding for the process of copyrighting their own work.

– Analyze the consequences and costs of unethical use of information and communication technology (for example, hacking, spamming, consumer fraud, virus setting, intrusion); identify ways of addressing those risks.

– Use programs and websites responsibly, efficiently, and ethically.

– Serve as a mentor for others who want to use information technology.

STRAND 4.1: SKILLS

STANDARD 4: Pursue personal and aesthetic growth

INDICATOR 4.1.1: **Read, view, and listen for pleasure and personal growth.**

– Read, view, and listen to learn, to solve problems, and to explore many different ideas.

– Routinely read, view, and listen for personal enjoyment.

– For personal growth and learning take advantage of opportunities available within the community, including classes, lectures, author presentations, museums, public library programming, and arts performances.

INDICATOR 4.1.2: **Read widely and fluently to make connections with self, the world, and previous reading.**

– Read, view, and use fiction and nonfiction to enrich understanding of real-world concepts.

– Derive multiple perspectives on the same themes by comparing across different works.

– Read widely to develop a global perspective and understand different cultural contexts.

– Read to support and challenge their own points of view.

INDICATOR 4.1.3: **Respond to literature and creative expressions of ideas in various formats and genres.**

– Express new ideas gained through information presented in various formats and connect the ideas to the human experience.

– Identify universal themes in literature and other creative forms of expression, and analyze different cultural approaches to those themes.

INDICATOR 4.1.4: **Seek information for personal learning in a variety of formats and genres.**

– Explore real-world genres (movie reviews, editorials, consumer reports, game tips and strategies, career information).

– Find information about personal interests independently, using the same criteria and strategies used to seek for academic information seeking.

INDICATOR 4.1.5: **Connect ideas to own interests and previous knowledge and experience.**

– Connect new ideas and understandings to future needs and interests that relate to college, careers, and personal lives.

– Reflect on changes in personal goals, reading preferences, personal interests, and knowledge base throughout the high school experience.

(continues on page 112)

(continued from page 111)

INDICATOR 4.1.6: | **Organize personal knowledge in a way that can be called upon easily.**

- Connect new information to ideas previously learned by developing graphic organizers and taxonomies (hierarchical classifications) to link large concepts to related details.
- Identify the main ideas by seeing the pattern they present (for example, cause and effect, growth or change over time).
- Standardize personal note-taking systems so that main ideas and personal responses (emotional reactions, questions) are incorporated.

INDICATOR 4.1.7: | **Use social networks and information tools to gather and share information.**

- Address real-world problems and issues by using information and communication technology tools to gather, evaluate, and use information from different sources, analyze findings, draw conclusions, and create solutions.
- Use telecommunication to search for and identify potential work, college, or other opportunities.
- Apply production strategies and technology tools to design products to meet personal needs.
- Participate in the social interchange of ideas through book discussions, interest groups, and online sharing.
- Participate responsibly and safely in social networks using appropriate tools to collaborate, as well as to share ideas and knowledge.

INDICATOR 4.1.8: | **Use creative and artistic formats to express personal learning.**

- Create original products to reflect personal interpretations of information and construction of new knowledge using multiple formats.
- Use a range of technology tools to produce sophisticated and creative renditions of personal learning.

ACTION EXAMPLE: GRADE 11–12

GRADE: 11–12

LIBRARY CONTEXT:

- ☐ Fixed
- ☑ Flexible
- ☐ Combination
- ☐ Individualized instruction
- ☐ Stand-alone lesson
- ☐ Lesson in a unit
- ☑ Multiple lessons in a unit

COLLABORATION CONTINUUM:

- ☐ None
- ☐ Limited
- ☐ Moderate
- ☑ Intensive

CONTENT TOPIC:

Relationship Between a Culture and its Folklore

ESTIMATED LESSON TIME:

Classes will be in the library for six sessions. The lessons taught by the SLMS will range in length from 10 to 30 minutes

Standards for the 21st-Century Learner Goals

STANDARD 4: Pursue personal and aesthetic growth.

SKILLS INDICATOR:

4.1.3 Respond to literature and creative expressions of ideas in various formats and genres.

BENCHMARKS:

– Express new ideas gained through information presented in various formats and connect the ideas to the human experience.

– Identify universal themes in literature and other creative forms of expression, and analyze different cultural approaches to those themes.

DISPOSITIONS INDICATOR:

3.2.3 Demonstrate teamwork by working productively with others.

RESPONSIBILITIES INDICATOR:

3.3.7 Respect the principles of intellectual freedom.

SELF-ASSESSMENT STRATEGIES INDICATOR:

2.4.2 Reflect on systematic process, and assess for completeness of investigation.

SCENARIO:

A world literature teacher e-mails the SLMS asking for a time to plan and schedule her classes into the library for the folktale unit. She and the SLMS have worked on this unit for the past two years, so this planning session will be devoted to mapping out the visits to the library and going over changes made during the evaluation at the conclusion of the unit last year. They set a time to plan.

The focus of the unit is to highlight the relationship between a culture and its stories. For this unit, the students read folktales from a particular culture, identify components of the society through the folktales, and conduct additional research on the culture. Then, with a partner, they write an original folktale that incorporates the characteristics of a folktale and what they have learned about the studied culture. In the past the final project was a slide presentation or a play based on the folktale.

During the planning session, the teacher and the SLMS start by reviewing the unit and determining the length of time the classes will need to meet in the library. These are juniors and seniors who have had several research experiences in the library. However, the teacher believes that they still need some instruction on effective

(continues on page 114)

(continued from page 113)

searches using the online databases and choosing the best websites for the information needed. Instruction in the classroom will focus on identifying characteristics of folktales, determining the common components of a culture (morals, values, way of life, etc.), developing questions, and using MLA format for the "works cited" list. The SLMS will focus on the available resources for the project, search strategies for online databases, and evaluation of websites, and will act as a consultant in the research process.

The teacher has expressed some dissatisfaction with the final products from the previous year. The SLMS (who has been advocating the use of picture books in the classroom) suggests that a picture book would be a good product for this type of assignment. She offers to work with the student teams as each writes and illustrates a picture book version of their original folktale. The teacher agrees that a picture book might prove more interesting to the students and decides to try it as a product this year.

The teacher and SLMS decide that six days in the library will be sufficient for this unit and set the schedule. They also schedule a second planning session to review the plans for each day in the library, design exit passes to assess student progress, and determine the criteria for rubrics to assess note taking, the final product, and work with a partner.

CONNECTION TO LOCAL OR STATE STANDARDS:

Content Standard for Grade 11 Language Arts: Describe literary contributions of various cultures.

Content Standard for Grade 12 Language Arts: Compare and contrast the literary contributions of various cultures.

OVERVIEW:

Juniors and seniors in a world literature class examine world cultures through the lens of a culture's folktales. The essential question is: How do folktales reflect a country's culture? In particular, the students (1) analyze how folktales convey a society's morals and values and (2) apply their knowledge by creating a literary piece in the folktale genre and reflecting aspects of the culture.

FINAL PRODUCT:

Student pairs collaborate on the creation of an original folktale that incorporates the values of a particular cultural group and embodies elements of the folktale genre. Each pair shares its work with the class as a picture book.

LIBRARY LESSONS:

Students learn to locate folktales, find information in online databases and websites about a specific cultural group, and create picture books from their original folktales.

ASSESSMENT

Product: Teacher, SLMS, and students use instructor-created rubrics to assess the folktales and the picture books. Criteria used to examine the quality of the new folktales include use of literary elements and motifs, development of story sense, and incorporation of cultural elements. Criteria used to examine the quality of the picture books will include several broad areas, such as organization of content, creative interpretation of material, and audience appeal and appropriateness.

Process: Teacher and SLMS examine student notes, exit passes, website evaluations, and works cited to determine whether (1) information gathered uses a variety of sources, (2) notes accurately reflect cultural components, (3) websites have been evaluated to meet criteria for acceptable websites, and (4) works cited meet requirements for number and types of sources, and have been correctly cited using MLA format.

Student self-questioning:

– Do the notes that I took while reading six folktales accurately reflect the components of their culture?
– Do the notes that I took during my research on my assigned culture accurately answer my questions?
– Did I make good choices in the sources of information I used, including the websites?
– Do my citations follow MLA format?

– Does my final product include the characteristics of a folktale and include cultural components?

– How well did I contribute to the creation of the final product?

– How well did I work with my partner?

INSTRUCTIONAL PLAN

Resources students will use:

- ■ Online subscription database(s)
- ■ Websites
- ■ Books
- ■ Reference
- ☐ Nonprint
- ☐ Periodicals/newspapers
- ☐ Other (list)

INSTRUCTION/ACTIVITIES

Direct Instruction:

Folklore index — Read a folktale from a Native American tribe to the class. Discuss what can be learned about the culture and identify the characteristics of a folktale.

Search strategies for online databases – Review the available online databases that will be appropriate for this assignment. Provide students with a handout highlighting search strategy tips (Boolean operators, nesting, limiting, expanding, keyword vs. subject heading, sorting results, etc.).

Evaluation of websites – Introduce the website evaluation rubric and discuss the criteria for choosing an appropriate website.

Characteristics of picture books – Using the folktale that was read when introducing the assignment, identify the characteristics of a picture book (abundance of illustrations, importance of illustrations in telling the story, less text, author notes, etc.).

Modeling and guided practice:

Folklore index – Introduce the library's folklore index which identifies folktales, their cultural group or native country, and the collection where the folktale can be found.

Search strategies for online databases – Demonstrate the various strategies from the handout on one of the subscription databases to locate articles about the same Native American tribe.

Evaluation of websites – Using the website evaluation rubric, the students as a class rate three websites on the Native American culture group used previously.

Characteristics of picture books – Students work with their partner to locate a folktale picture book from their chosen

culture. After they have identified the picture book's characteristics, they share their findings with the other students at their table.

Independent practice:

Folklore index – Students locate and read six folktales representing the culture or country they have chosen to investigate.

Search strategies for online databases – Students locate articles on their chosen culture using the demonstrated strategies. The students have the remainder of the class period plus the next day to get their articles.

Evaluation of websites – Students locate websites on their chosen culture and rate the sites using the website evaluation rubric. Based on their ratings, they choose the best two, and take notes to answer their questions.

Characteristics of picture books – Based on the information gathered and the folktales that they read about their chosen culture, the students write and illustrate an original folktale in the picture book format.

Sharing and reflecting:

Folklore index – Students work with their partners to compare the folktales they have located and read. They identify common components (morals, values, way of life, etc.) of their chosen cultural group.

Search strategies for online databases – Students complete an exit pass at the end of the two class periods. The exit pass lists each article and the search strategy used to find the article. The students also share the articles with their partner and compare the information gathered. They look for gaps and misinformation.

Evaluation of websites – Students turn in the website evaluation rubrics, indicating the reasons for rejecting or choosing each of the websites they located. They share the information they gathered from their chosen two with their partners while looking for gaps and misinformation.

Characteristics of picture books – The original picture books will be read to the class by the authors and illustrators. The class will have an opportunity to respond by identifying the cultural components and the characteristics of a picture book. The students will be asked to write a reflection on the process of writing and illustrating an original folktale, on how well they incorporated the cultural components into their folktale, and on working with a partner to complete the project.

ACTION EXAMPLE TEMPLATE

GRADE:

LIBRARY CONTEXT:

☐ Fixed

☐ Flexible

☐ Combination

☐ Individualized instruction

☐ Stand-alone lesson

☐ Lesson in a unit

☐ Multiple lessons in a unit

COLLABORATION CONTINUUM:

☐ None

☐ Limited

☐ Moderate

☐ Intensive

CONTENT TOPIC:

ESTIMATED LESSON TIME:

STANDARDS FOR THE 21st-CENTURY LEARNER GOALS

STANDARD:

BENCHMARK(S):

DISPOSITIONS INDICATOR(S):

RESPONSIBILITIES INDICATOR(S):

SELF-ASSESSMENT STRATEGIES INDICATOR(S):

SCENARIO:

CONNECTION TO LOCAL OR STATE STANDARDS

(List here relevant content, information literacy, and technology standards)

OVERVIEW:

FINAL PRODUCT:

LIBRARY LESSON(S):

ASSESSMENT:

PRODUCT

PROCESS

STUDENT SELF-QUESTIONING

INSTRUCTIONAL PLAN

RESOURCES STUDENTS WILL USE:

☐ Online subscription database(s)   ☐ Nonprint

☐ Websites   ☐ Periodicals/newspapers

☐ Books   ☐ Other (list)

☐ Reference

INSTRUCTION/ACTIVITIES:

DIRECT INSTRUCTION:

MODELING AND GUIDED PRACTICE:

INDEPENDENT PRACTICE:

SHARING AND REFLECTING:

8 LEARNING4LIFE (L4L)

A National Plan for Implementation of *Standards for the 21st-Century Learner* and *Empowering Learners: Guidelines for the School Library Media Program*

This implementation plan was created to support states, school systems, and individual schools preparing to implement the *Standards for the 21st-Century Learner* and *Empowering Learners: Guidelines for School Library Media Programs*. The plan will also increase awareness and understanding of the learning standards and guidelines and create a committed group of stakeholders with a shared voice.

While the learning standards and guidelines define what "should be" in terms of information literacy, research through guided inquiry, and the integration of technology in the traditional school context, they also acknowledge varied and new forms of teaching and learning in a social and global context. Foundational to this plan is the fundamental value of reading, core content, and mastery of skills that produce deep knowledge and understanding, as well as the portable skills that serve individuals for a lifetime, making them critical thinkers, problem solvers, and continually evolving learners. To this end, the implementation plan addresses the practical realization of these important skills and values as it

- identifies guiding principles and an overarching position and branding statement;
- identifies target audiences (internal and external);
- identifies training opportunities and resources;
- provides a communication plan;
- provides a plan for continuous feedback, evaluation, and sustainability;
- provides a plan for endorsements and support;
- provides supporting documents.

The plan is available online at www.ala.org/aasl/learning4life. For questions about the implementation plan, please contact Jennifer Habley, Manager, Programs and Affiliate Relations, jhabley@ala.org, (800) 545-2433 x 4383.

9 GLOSSARY

aesthetic growth: Process in which individuals develop the ability to think about and respond to artistic/aesthetic stimuli (Housen 1983).

assessment: Process of "collecting, analyzing, and reporting data" (Coatney 2003, 157) about student accomplishments and understandings throughout a learning experience. Forms of assessment include tests, observations, self-assessments, conferences, logs, graphic organizers, surveys, checklists, rubrics, and interviews (Wiggins and McTighe 2005, Harada and Yoshina 2005).

Diagnostic assessment is the use of formal or informal measurement tools to assess an individual's area of strengths and needs for purposes of identifying appropriate learning modifications or adaptations. Two examples of diagnostic assessment tools include running records (informal) and Weschler Intelligence Scale for Children (formal).

Formative assessment is ongoing and provides information about what students are learning and how that learning is taking place. It gives students feedback on their progress and provides teachers with feedback on the effectiveness of their instruction (Donham 2008, 266; Harada and Yoshina 2005, 1).

Summative assessment occurs at the end of the learning process and is intended to evaluate student performance. It also provides feedback that can be used to redesign learning experiences (Donham 2008, 266; Harada and Yoshina 2005, 1).

authentic assessment: Assessment techniques that require students to originate a response to a task or question, using knowledge in real-world ways, with genuine purposes, audiences, and situational variables; may include demonstrations, exhibits, portfolios, oral presentations, or essays (Donham 2008, 267; Wiggins and McTighe 2005, 337). Authentic assessment helps to measure how effectively students apply knowledge to the real world (Collins and O'Brien 2003, 33).

benchmark: Statement that provides a description of student knowledge expected at specific grades, ages, or developmental levels. Benchmarks are often used in conjunction with standards and provide concrete indicators of student understanding (NCREL 2002).

constructivism: Learning theory that suggests optimal learning occurs when individuals are actively engaged in authentic and meaningful tasks, and have opportunities to interpret and reflect on these interactions. As school library media specialists, the goal of instruction is not to inform, but rather to create situations in which students are able to "construct" new understandings (Brooks and Brooks 2001).

convergent thinking: Thinking that brings together information focused on solving a problem (especially solving a problem that has a single correct solution).

critical stance: Attitude or disposition toward learning in which students are positioned to develop an understanding of a topic or issue through objectivity, inquiry, hypothesis, analysis and evaluation, comparing and contrasting, and consideration of implications.

critical thinking: "Reasonable thinking that is focused on deciding what to believe or do" (Ennis 1987, 10). Critical thinking includes the ability to "set goals, to adjust strategies, to carry out tasks, to distinguish fact from opinion, to establish the authority of sources, to assess the accuracy and relevancy of information, and to detect bias and underlying assumptions" (Thomas 2004, 119).

diagnostic assessment: See assessment.

differentiated instruction: Teaching theory based on the belief that instructional approaches should vary and be adapted for individual and diverse students in classrooms. The intent of differentiating instruction is "to maximize each student's growth and individual success by meeting each student where he or she is, and assisting in the learning process" (Hall 2002, para. 2).

digital literacy: Ability to understand, evaluate, create, and integrate information in multiple digital formats via the computer and Internet (Gilster 1997).

direct instruction: General term for the explicit teaching of a skill set. The most commonly identified steps of direct instruction include introduction/review, presenting new material, guided practice, independent practice, weekly/monthly review, and feedback/corrections (Collins and O'Brien 2003, 107).

dispositions: Ongoing beliefs and attitudes that guide thinking and intellectual behavior. Often referred to as habits of mind or tendencies to respond to situations in a certain way (Katz 1988).

divergent thinking: Creative production or elaboration of ideas; associated with elements of creative problem solving.

emotional resilience: Ability to "spring back emotionally after suffering through difficult and stressful times" (Mills and Dombeck 2005, 1). Emotional resilience requires setting realistic and attainable expectations and goals, good problem solving skills, persistence and determination, learning from past mistakes, and an optimistic attitude (Mills and Dombeck 2005).

formative assessment: See assessment.

global perspective: Individual's awareness and understanding of the changing world with regard to global issues, culture, and connections, and the individual's roles and responsibilities as a member of the global community (Collins, Czarra, and Smith 2003).

guided practice: Instructional strategy that enables students to "practice a new skill or strategy while the teacher provides close monitoring, immediate feedback, and assistance as needed" (Collins and O'Brien 2003, 160).

higher-level thinking/questioning: Ability to think and question in a manner that requires consideration and application of complex concepts, problem solving skills, and reflection. Bloom's Taxonomy identifies a hierarchy of six levels of thinking, with the top three (analysis, synthesis, and evaluation) classified as higher-order thinking skills (Bloom et al. 1956).

information literacy: Skill set needed to find, retrieve, analyze, and use information (ACRL 2003).

independent practice: Instructional strategy that enables students to "practice newly learned content, skills, or strategies on their own with no direct teacher assistance" (Collins and O'Brien 2003, 175).

inquiry: Stance toward learning in which the learner is engaged in asking questions and finding answers, not simply accumulating facts presented by someone else that have no relation to previous learning or new understanding. Inquiry follows a continuum of learning experiences, from simply discovering a new idea or an answer to a question to following a complete inquiry process (Kuhlthau, Maniotes, and Caspari 2007).

lower-level thinking/questioning: Use of basic skills (such as recall, rote memorization, and simple comprehension) to think and question. Bloom's Taxonomy identifies a hierarchy of six levels of thinking; the lowest three are knowledge, comprehension, application (Bloom et al. 1956).

media literacy: Ability to "access, analyze, evaluate and create messages in a variety of forms—from print to video to the Internet. Media literacy builds an understanding of the role of media in society as well as essential skills of inquiry and self-expression necessary for citizens of a democracy" (Center for Media Literacy n.d.).

metacognition: Act of thinking about thinking. Metacognition challenges students to consider and regulate their own learning. Metacognitive strategies include assessing or reviewing current and previous knowledge, identifying gaps in that knowledge, planning gap-filling strategies, determining the relevance of new information, and possibly revising beliefs or understandings about the subject (NCREL 2002).

modeling: Instructional strategy in which the teacher demonstrates to the student the behaviors, skills, or competencies that students are to learn, with the expectation that the students will copy the model. Modeling often involves thinking aloud or talking about how to work through a task (Collins and O'Brien 2003, NCREL 2002).

multiple intelligences: Cognitive theory developed by Howard Gardner that proposes that intelligence is not a unitary or fixed trait, but a collection of different abilities with neurological foundations (Collins and O'Brien 2003, 230). Gardner proposed nine intelligences: linguistic, musical, logical-mathematical, visual-spatial, bodily-kinesthetic, intrapersonal, interpersonal, naturalist, and existential (Gardner 1999).

responsibilities: Common behaviors used by independent learners in researching, investigating, and problem solving.

scaffolding: Instructional strategy "in which a more skilled teaching partner adjusts the assistance he or she provides to fit the child's current level of performance. More support is offered when the task is new; less is provided as the child's competence increases, fostering the child's autonomy and independent mastery" (Callison 2006, 523). The gradual withdrawal of support is generated through instruction, questioning, modeling, feedback, etc. (Collins and O'Brien 2003, 312).

self-assessment: Assessment technique in which learners develop internal standards, compare their performance, behaviors, or thoughts to those standards, and then use their observations to improve learning. Self-assessment requires students to engage in reflection of their own learning and to focus not just on the task or the product, but also on the process. Self-assessment tools include journaling, rating scales, check lists, questionnaires, and rubrics (Donham 2008).

social networking: Ability to "connect, collaborate and form virtual communities via the computer and/or Internet. Social networking web sites are those that provide this opportunity to interact via interactive web applications. Sites that allow visitors to send emails, post comments, build web content and/or take part in live chats are all considered to be social networking sites. These kinds of sites have come to be collectively referred to as "Web 2.0" and are considered the next generation of the Internet because they allow users to interact and participate in a way that we couldn't before" (YALSA 2008).

standards: Statements of what students should know and be able to demonstrate. Various standards have been developed by national organizations, state departments of education, individual districts, and schools (NCREL 2002).

summative assessment: See assessment,

technology literacy: Ability to responsibly use appropriate technology to communicate, solve problems, and access, manage, integrate, evaluate, and create information to improve learning in all subject areas and to acquire lifelong knowledge and skills in the twenty-first century (SETDA n.d.).

textual literacy: Ability to read, write, analyze, and evaluate textual works of literature and personal and professional documents.

visual literacy: Ability to "understand and use images, including the ability to think, learn, and express oneself in terms of images" (Braden and Hortin 1982, 41).

Web 2.0: Trend in Web design and development that has transformed the way individuals use the Internet, fostering creativity, interaction, and collaboration through Web applications such as blogs, wikis, RSS feeds, and social networks.

writing process: Pedagogical term referring to a set of steps an individual takes while writing. They include: prewriting, writing, revising, editing, and publishing.

10 REFERENCE LIST

American Association of School Librarians. 2007. *Standards for the 21st-century learner.* <www.ala.org/ala/aasl/aasl proftools/learningstandards /AASL_Learning Standards. pdf> (accessed August 14, 2008).

Anderson, Lorin W., and David R. Krathwohl, eds. 2001. *A taxonomy for learning, teaching, and assessing: A revision of Bloom's taxonomy of educational objectives.* New York: Addison Wesley Longman.

Association of College and Research Libraries. 2003. Introduction to information literacy. <www.ala.org/ala/mgrps/divs/acrl/issues/infolit/infolitoverview/introtoinfolit/introinfolit.cfm> (accessed December 10, 2008).

Bloom, Benjamin S., M. D. Engelhart, E. J. Furst, W. H. Hill, and D. R. Krathwohl. 1956. *Taxonomy of educational objectives. Handbook 1: Cognitive domain.* New York: McKay.

Braden, R. A., and J. A. Horton. 1982. Identifying the theoretical foundations of visual literacy. *Journal of Visual/Verbal Languaging* 2, 37–42.

Brooks, J. G., and M. G. Brooks. 2001. *In search of understanding: The case for constructivist classrooms.* New Jersey: Merrill Prentice Hall.

Callison, D. 2006. Scaffolding. *The blue book on information age inquiry, instruction and literacy.* D. Callison and L. Preddy, eds. Westport, CT: Libraries Unlimited, 523–26.

Center for Media Literacy. n.d. Media literacy: A definition ...and more. <www.medialit.org/reading_room/rr2def.php> (accessed December 11, 2008).

Claxton, Guy. 2007. Expanding young peoples' capacity to learn. *British Journal of Educational Studies* 55, no.2, 115–34.

Coatney, S. 2003. Assessment for learning. *Curriculum connections through the library.* B. K. Stripling and S. Hughes-Hassell, eds. Westport, CT: Libraries Unlimited, 157–68.

Collins, H. T., F. R. Czarra, and A. F. Smith. 2003. Guidelines for global and international studies education: Challenges, culture, connections. <www.globaled.org/guidelines> (accessed December 11, 2008).

Collins, J. W., III, and N. P. O'Brien, eds. 2003. *The Greenwood dictionary of education.* Westport, CT: Greenwood.

Costa, Arthur L., and Bena Kallick. 2000. *Discovering and exploring habits of mind.* Alexandria, VA: ASCD.

Donham, J. 2008. *Enhancing teaching and learning: A leadership guide for school library media specialists.* 2nd ed. New York: Neal-Schuman.

Ennis, R. H. 1987. A taxonomy of critical thinking dispositions and abilities. *Teaching thinking skills: Theory and practice.* J. B. Baron and R. J. Sternberg, eds. New York: W.H. Freeman, 9–26.

Gardner, H. 1999. *Intelligence reframed: Multiple intelligences for the 21st century.* New York: Basic Books.

Gilster, P. 1997. *Digital literacy.* New York: Wiley.

Hall, T. 2002. *Differentiated instruction.* National Center on Accessing the General Curriculum. <www.cast.org/publications/ncac/ncac_diffinstruc.html> (accessed December 9, 2008).

Harada, V. H., and J. M. Yoshina. 2005. *Assessing learning: Librarians and teachers as partners.* Westport, CT: Libraries Unlimited.

Housen, A. 1983. *The eye of the beholder: Measuring aesthetic development.* Unpublished doctoral dissertation. Harvard Graduate School of Education, Boston.

Katz, L. G. 1988. What should young children be doing? *American Educator* 12, no.2, 28–33, 44–45.

Katz, Lillian G. 2000. Dispositions as educational goals. ERIC Digest. ERIC Identifier: ED363454. <www.eric.ed.gov/ERICDocs/data/ericdocs2sql/content_storage_01/0000019b/80/13/28/ca.pdf> (accessed December 14, 2008).

Kuhlthau, C. C., L. K. Maniotes, and A. K. Caspari. 2007. *Guided inquiry: Learning in the 21st century.* Westport, CT: Libraries Unlimited.

Montiel-Overall, P. 2006. Teacher and teacher-librarian collaboration: Moving toward integration. *Teacher Librarian* 34, no.2, 28–33.

Mills, H. and M. Dombeck. 2005. Attitudes and skills of emotional resilience. <www.mentalhelp.net/poc/view_doc.php?type=doc&id=5779&cn=298> (accessed December 12, 2008).

New York City School Library System. Information Fluency Continuum. <http://schools.nycenet.edu/offices/teachlearn/sls/INFO_FLUENCY_CONT_K12Final.pdf> (accessed December 11, 2008).

North Central Regional Educational Laboratory. 2002. Glossary of education terms and acronyms. <www.ncrel.org/sdrs/areas/misc/glossary.htm> (accessed December 17, 2008).

Perkins, David N. 1992. *Smart schools: From training memories to educating minds.* New York: Free Press.

State Educational Technology Directors Association, Technology Literacy Assessment Work Group. Technology literacy. <www.nde.state.ne.us/techcen/Technology Literacy.html> (accessed December 11, 2008).

Thomas, N. P. 2004. *Information literacy and information skills instruction: Applying research to practice in the school library media center.* 2nd ed. Westport, CT: Libraries Unlimited.

Wiggins, G. P., and J. McTighe. 2005. *Understanding by design.* Alexandria, VA: ASCD.

Young Adult Library Services Association. 2008. Teens and social networking in school and public libraries: A toolkit for librarians and library workers. <www.ala.org/ala/mgrps/divs/yalsa/profdev/SocialNetworkingToolkit_Jan08.pdf> (accessed December 11, 2008).